# I Want to Say a Few Words: How To Craft a Heartfelt Eulogy for a Loved One's Funeral

A Simple Step-by-Step Process, Packed with Eulogy Writing Ideas, Help & Advice from a Professional Eulogy Writer

## Peter Billingham

Randan Press

© 2023 Peter Billingham. All rights reserved.

Peter Billingham asserts the moral right identified as the author of this work under the Copyright, Designs and Patents Act 1988

Cover designed by GetCovers

ISBN – Paperback 978-1-913911-46-1

ISBN – eBook - 978-1-913911-45-4

ISBN – Audio Book – 978-1-913911-47-8

This book is sold subject to the condition that it shall not, by way of trade or otherwise, be lent, resold, hired out, or otherwise circulated without the publisher's prior consent in any form of binding or cover other than that in which it is published and without a similar condition including this condition being imposed on the subsequent publisher.

No part of this publication may be reproduced, stored in a retrieval system, distributed, or transmitted in any form or by any means, including photocopying, recording, or other electronic or mechanical methods, without the prior written permission of the author.

Typeset in – EB Garamond – Formatted on Atticus

First edition independently published under the pen name – Randan Press 2023

For permission requests, visit the author's website at www.peterbillingham.com. Or write to or www.memorablewords.co.uk.

# Dedication

To the families who have entrusted me with the honour of writing a eulogy for their deeply loved ones, I extend my heartfelt thanks and gratitude. I deeply appreciate your confidence in my abilities as a speechwriter and celebrant.

To the hundreds of individuals whose lives I've had the privilege to illuminate and whose coffins I have stood beside, thank you. The honour of learning about you, crafting your eulogy, and sharing the unique stories of your lives is one I carry with great respect.

Thank you.

# CONTENTS

Foreword ... 1

1. Introduction ... 5
2. How This Toolkit Helps Craft Your Heartfelt Eulogy ... 7
3. What Is The Simple Four-Step Process? ... 11

STEP ONE: RESEARCH ... 15

4. Worksheet 1 - Basic Information ... 17
5. Discovering Character Traits and Personality Themes ... 21
6. Worksheet 2 - Discovering Personality Themes and Character Traits ... 25
7. What Four Key Questions Rekindle Emotional Memories? ... 29
8. Worksheet 3 - Four Key Questions ... 31
9. Imagining Their Perfect Day ... 37
10. Worksheet 4 – Perfect Day Planner ... 39

STEP TWO: DRAFT ... 43

11. From Memories to Manuscript: How to Start Drafting Your Eulogy ... 45
12. Why Use This Simple Eulogy Outline? ... 49
13. How Many Words Will You Need To Write? ... 53
14. Turning Your Memories into Mini-Stories ... 55
15. Worksheet 5 – Memory 1 – Key Theme A ... 60
16. Worksheet 6 – Memory 2 – Key Theme B ... 62
17. Worksheet 7 – Memory 3 – Key Theme C ... 64

| | | |
|---|---|---|
| 18. | How To Write The Conclusion | 67 |
| 19. | Worksheet 8 - Writing The Conclusion | 71 |
| 20. | How To Write The Introduction | 73 |
| 21. | Worksheet 9 - Writing The Introduction | 79 |

| | | |
|---|---|---|
| STEP THREE: EDIT | | 81 |
| 22. | How Does Editing Craft Your First Draft into a Heartfelt Eulogy? | 83 |
| 23. | Worksheet 10 – Bringing Your Words Together | 87 |

| | | |
|---|---|---|
| STEP FOUR: REHEARSAL | | 93 |
| 24. | Why Is Rehearsing Your Eulogy a Key Step in the Process? | 95 |
| 25. | How to Stand Strong When Saying Your Words | 99 |
| 26. | Closing Thoughts | 103 |

| | | |
|---|---|---|
| Common Questions & Bonus Resources | | 105 |
| 27. | Common Questions & Bonus Resources Contents | 107 |
| 28. | Bonus Worksheet 1 – The Lifeline Exercise | 113 |
| 29. | Bonus Worksheet 2 – Life Lessons and Legacy | 117 |
| 30. | Bonus Worksheet 3 – 10 Overriding Life Themes | 119 |
| 31. | Bonus Worksheet 4 – 36 Extra Memory Prompt Questions | 135 |
| 32. | Bonus Worksheet 5 – 26 Quotations For Telling A Life Story | 139 |
| 33. | Bonus Worksheet 6 – Family & Friends Questionnaire | 143 |
| 34. | Bespoke Eulogy Writing Solutions | 155 |
| 35. | Acknowledgements | 159 |
| 36. | About the author | 161 |
| 37. | Disclaimer | 163 |

# Foreword

When I grow up, I want to be a firefighter!

Or perhaps, no, I'll be a teacher, actor or engineer instead.

You don't dream that one day you'll grow up and write heartfelt words about people you've never met that have died.

But that's what happened. That is what I do.

I am a eulogy speechwriter and celebrant. It is a vocation that brings meaning and purpose to my life, by being able to voice the way someone deeply feels into words. All my life experiences in leading organisations, writing, and public speaking to date now help me help others.

On a frequent basis, I find myself invited into people's homes and lives to help them during a time of deep sadness when someone they love has died.

A funeral is being planned. Some words about the person they love will be need to be said at that funeral service.

The air in the room is as heavy with the scent of fresh flowers as it is with the uncertainty of what happens next.

I look around me. I've seen the same scene hundreds of times before. Digital messages replace most person-to-person communication today. But handwritten sympathy cards fill shelves, window ledges, and bookcases. Each simple message bringing comfort and care through ink on paper rather than text on a screen.

A small group of grieving people look to me to help them in their time of loss.

And then I hear '**the phrase**.'

It's a phrase filled with many emotions - sadness and loss, gratitude, perhaps some guilt, adoration, but above all, love.

Hundreds of times I've heard the phrase, 'I want to say a few words at the funeral.' Then it seems always followed by, 'but.'

But:

- What would I say?

- How would I even start to write a few words?

- Do I have the emotional strength to stand up on the day and speak?

- It's something I want to do for them. Could I?

Speaking at a loved one's funeral can be difficult, especially with the doubts and fears that come with it.

A while ago, sitting in a cafe, I happened to see a man I knew. Let me call him John. I led the funeral service of his father, who had died three years before.

John is a quiet, even reserved man, not a 'life and soul of the party' personality. Certainly not the kind of person who would jump to speak in public. Despite John's fears, he was determined to honour his dad's life by saying a few words at his funeral. John and his dad shared a special relationship. Yes, he was his dad, but they were the best of friends, too. They shared a deep love of supporting a local football team and rarely, if ever, had missed sitting in the same season ticket seats, side by side, for decades. It was a bond that kept them close for life. And now in death.

So I helped John write those words. Though not formalised as it is now in this book, it was the same step-by-step process you now hold in your hands.

The day of the funeral arrived. John, through tears and emotion, and stopping and starting a few times to compose himself, spoke those words of love about his dad and the team they loved. He wore the team football shirt that day. What made it poignant was when, in his eulogy, he told everyone that his dad was wearing his too.

John was so affirming and supportive of the help I'd given him. Confiding in me that three years later still had an overwhelming sense of gratitude for having had the guidance which gave him the strength to voice his feelings that day.

My wish with this book is to do the same for you. Through the power of words on a page, I hope to be a compassionate companion, supporting and guiding you. The aim is not just to write a few words, but to give you the steps to find a sense and feeling of accomplishment which can help you in the years to come.

In this compassionate guide, I will lead you through a simple four-step process.

We begin with '**Research**.' Here you will spend most of your time gathering meaningful memories and bringing to mind the unique person your loved one was. '**Drafting**' guides you on how to structure these memories into mini-stories. In '**Editing**', you'll refine your words, ensuring that your 'few words' feel authentic and sincere. Finally, '**Rehearsing**' gives you all the help you will need to deliver your heartfelt eulogy with confidence, even during your grief. Many times I hear from people who complete the 'Research' stage they collect far more information than they could ever use in a short eulogy. But that doesn't matter as pouring over old letters, photos, and mementos bring back a wealth of happy memories. These notes and thoughts become a treasure trove of memories stored away for future generations. They tell me it was overwhelming, but was also incredibly therapeutic somehow.

I imagine you are thinking writing a few words about your loved one is a monumental task, especially when you are feeling the pain of loss.

It's not uncommon for people in that same situation to spend countless hours staring at a blank page. It's a simple four-step process - '**Research**', '**Draft**', '**Edit**', and '**Rehearse**' that saves you having to worry about what to do first, and how to do it. The words taking shape more quickly than you thought possible. This workbook and worksheets makes writing a lasting and meaningful eulogy for your loved one's funeral manageable.

So, this book is for those people who want to say a few words.

This book is for you if you find yourself in the same place, asking the same questions.

But it is also for me.

We all die. One day I will die, and when I do, I want to leave behind more than just memories. After penning countless eulogies for others, I wonder who will say a few words about me? All the hundreds of life stories I've told, what will someone say about the story of my life? 'In the end, we'll all become stories,' wrote Margaret Atwood. She's right. Stories someone tells at a funeral.

I've spent many hours and poured all the experience of the years into this eulogy writing process. I would like to give someone who loves me the tools they need, if they so chose, to help say a few words about me.

My aim in writing this practical step-by-step guide with no steps missing is simple: if you want to say a few words at the funeral of a loved one, now you can.

Everything you need to move past your doubts and fears, and confidently share your words of love and remembrance, is in here.

I hope the experience of my life, the skills, help, and advice I have gathered and shared in these pages provide the support you need during your difficult time. I want you to say a few words at the funeral of your loved one.

Peter Billingham – 2023

# Chapter 1

## INTRODUCTION

CRAFTING A HEARTFELT EULOGY for a loved one's funeral is the hardest speech you will make. Saying 'a few words' at their funeral service feels daunting, overwhelming and an impossible challenge. But to say those few words at the celebration of their life is perhaps the last and most special gift you can give them.

I am sorry someone you love has died. I'm sorry for your loss.

There are many reasons deep inside why we want to remember and celebrate a life with words. To put into voice our feelings of sadness, gratitude, and love. To tell the person, and those who will be there on the day, how irreplaceable they are. How from now on life will never be the same without them.

It's only a few words. But it's never 'just a few words,' is it? They could be the most important words you will ever say.

You will feel the weight of time pressing upon you to write your words. The funeral service is perhaps only a few days away. Asking yourself, will I have enough time? I understand the concern you may feel when trying to come up with the right words. Don't worry, everything you will need to craft a heartfelt eulogy is here in this toolkit.

**But where do you start?**

Writing and delivering a eulogy is not like any other speech. There is a lot at stake. It is a complex combination of emotions you experience, wanting to say something heartfelt and meaningful in a few words.

Maybe you are thinking:

- I want to do my best for them.

- I want to make them proud.

- I want to do justice to how special they were.

This eulogy writing toolkit, step-by-step, will be your guide through **researching, drafting, editing** and **rehearsing** a heartfelt eulogy. I've created a simple, easy to follow process to guide you how to say a few words, even if you've never written or given a speech in public before.

**When you follow the four-step process in this toolkit:**

You will write words that are memorable, personal, and unique. There are no fill-in-the-blank eulogy templates here. Your loved one was unique. How can the empty blank spaces speak of their unique personality? They can't. But your crafted words can.

You will be prepared to deliver the words as best as you can on the day of the funeral.

Afterwards, you will experience feeling you have done the best you could to honour their life.

I know this process works. Why? It's a tried and tested plan that has helped me write hundreds of meaningful and memorable eulogies.

While it may be the hardest speech you will ever make, you now have in your hands the path to follow, helping you step by step to do the best you can to craft a heartfelt eulogy for your loved one's funeral.

# Chapter 2

# How This Toolkit Helps Craft Your Heartfelt Eulogy

**Four Key Ways This Toolkit Helps Craft Your Heartfelt Eulogy.**

## 1 – It will give you a complete process from start to saying a few words at the funeral.

Creating a eulogy is a complicated task with many parts. This eulogy writing toolkit has ten practical worksheets and six bonus worksheets. Along with a wealth of ideas, expert help and advice, they will help you complete every aspect of writing the eulogy on time, with results you will be proud of.

## 2 – It will save you an incredible amount of time.

Each step in this eulogy writing toolkit helps you prepare a heartfelt eulogy for a loved one's funeral. By completing the worksheets and following the instructions, you'll save time and guesswork. This process eases your anxiety and doubt in writing the words.

## 3 – It will help you write a unique eulogy for your loved one.

Your loved one is a unique individual. So there are no fill-in-the-blank eulogy templates here. However, there are many examples for you to follow. By completing each step, you can adapt and add sections to suit their age, life story, and legacy. Writing some words about them. This process works regardless of the length of the words you want to say. From a short, succinct tribute to a longer, detailed and all-encompassing eulogy.

## 4 – It will bring you comfort and peace of mind.

The step-by-step process guides you, bringing to mind stories, memories and thoughts of your loved one, perhaps in a way that you have never done before. We rarely take the time to write stories about people we love. Now you can.

**But there is something else that happens as you spend concentrated time remembering your loved one.**

Many people tell me completing the research in the step-by-step process was cathartic and healing in a time of their deep loss and sadness. Committed to saying something at the funeral, they didn't know what to do first. They felt stuck and confused, compounding their feelings of anxiety about saying a few words. But after spending focused, guided time thinking and writing some thoughts, it brought back happy memories and made them feel confident to go forward and write a eulogy. It brought them happiness in times when joy was hard to find.

*Remember, take care of yourself too.*

As you gather your thoughts and recall your memories, it's only natural you will feel a wide range of emotions - from sadness and grief to happiness and joy. Writing a eulogy can be emotionally challenging, and it's OK to take breaks or step away from the task if you need to.

Now, in your hands, you have the tools you to create something special to say about your loved one. Now you can 'say a few memorable and meaningful words' at their funeral.

## What You Will Find In The Toolkit?

The Eulogy Writing Toolkit is divided into four Steps:

- **Research**
- **Draft**
- **Edit**
- **Rehearse**

Work through these four Steps in order. Each section includes the what, why, and how of writing the eulogy with examples and worksheets to complete.

**But that's not all you will find in this eulogy writing toolkit.**

In the **Common Questions & Bonus Resources** section, is a wealth of comprehensive supporting information I've learned and collected over the last ten years or more. The extra resources and examples provide you with writing ideas, expert help, and insightful advice I've gained as a professional eulogy writer. As well as the skills, experience and knowledge of decades of public speaking and years at Toastmasters International.

**The most important thing is to start.**

Procrastination will nudge you to wait until you can find lots of free time. You won't find it. We often underestimate what a small amount of time allocated over a few days can achieve. Don't leave it to the last moment to wait for inspiration. Start working through the steps today.

# Chapter 3

# What Is The Simple Four-Step Process?

## What Is The Simple Four-Step Process?

Creating a eulogy is like weaving a tapestry of memories, each thread carrying a piece of your loved one's life that you've come to cherish. This chapter is here to walk you through the simple, four-step process. This easy-to-follow guide, although simple, leaves plenty of room for the unique bond you shared with your loved one whose life you're honouring through a heartfelt eulogy.

Remember: there's no single 'right' way to express your loss. The steps that follow should be thought of as a framework to guide you. Your journey will involve looking back, self-reflection, and the courage to put your emotions into words. So, let's begin this journey together, starting with the first and crucial step: research.

**Step One—Research**

This is the first and important step. This section will prompt you to answer questions and recall memories.

It will be here you spend most of your time. Using questionnaires, worksheets and reflective activities, you will gather lots of memories, notes and ideas. You will narrow down the key memories into stories you can then use in your eulogy.

You begin collecting factual information. Then you move on to the personal characteristics of the person, helping you recall stories and memories of how they influenced your life and how they enjoyed their life. The more information, and the more specific the details you have at hand, the easier it will be when you move on to step two.

**Step Two—Draft**

Here we get the beginnings of the words for your eulogy.

Writing a few words of eulogy to say begins by getting words on a page. It is bringing the memories out of your head and into a place where you can decide which ones you are going to use when you speak.

**Remember this important point.**

Don't worry about sentences, grammar or getting it 'right' at this stage.

Procrastination and perfectionism can stop the process before it's begun. This stage is about taking the draft ideas, collating them and putting them together in a simple structure. This step encourages you to draft the words, ready to move on to edit and refine them in step three.

**Step Three—Edit**

This section shapes the words of the eulogy in a way that feels natural and sounds right when spoken aloud.

Don't expect getting your few words the way you want them first draft. All books, articles and speeches go through many edits and rewrites. Your few words will be the same.

You write your words to speak, so we do not want them to read like an English essay or magazine article. It's writing the final version to sound as you speak. Finish this step and you are ready to rehearse the words in step four.

**Step Four—Rehearsal**

Don't overlook this crucial step. Practicing the words as much as possible will make a big difference on the day.

What will help settle your nerves and emotions on the day is the rehearsal you put in beforehand. There are a few simple ways you can help yourself prepare for saying the words.

Don't skip rehearsal. It will reward you tenfold the time spent here in saying your few words at the funeral.

In conclusion, this Four-Step Process is a practical guide to how to craft a heartfelt eulogy. By researching memories and stories, drafting your initial thoughts, editing for clarity and tone, and rehearsing for confidence, you'll be well-prepared to deliver a heartfelt eulogy at your loved one's funeral.

# Takeaways and Actions from Introduction

## Important Takeaways:

- A eulogy is a special gift you can give to the loved one you've lost - it's not only 'a few words'.

- Writing a eulogy is different from other speeches, carrying a complex mix of emotions.

- This eulogy writing toolkit is here to help guide you through the process.

- Your loved one was unique - your eulogy should reflect that uniqueness.

- The toolkit is divided into four steps: Research, Draft, Edit, and Rehearse.

- Writing a eulogy can also be a healing process.

- Start the process as soon as you can, working in small bits of time if needed.

## Action Points:

1. Acknowledge the weight of this task and be gentle with yourself throughout the process.

2. Begin Step One in the four-step process: Research.

3. Use the toolkit's worksheets and extra resources to help you through each step.

4. Write any thoughts or memories that come to mind, even if they don't seem to fit in right away.

5. You will find at the back of this workbook are pages for notes. As you work through the steps, memories, thoughts and stories will come to mind. As they do, jot them down. You can come back to them later, as well as building up a storehouse of memories as a keepsake.

# STEP ONE: RESEARCH

# Chapter 4

# Worksheet 1 - Basic Information

## Worksheet 1 - Basic Information

Start by gathering the basic information for the funeral or memorial service. Yes, lots of this information you will know, but starting to write helps words begin to flow. Fill in as many details as you can, but don't worry if there are gaps, you can come back and add more information as you know them. Skip ahead to the sections you can answer.

In this worksheet are also some valuable and helpful tips and advice as you think about the service and speaking that day. Don't miss these out. Experience of leading hundreds of funerals has taught me these lessons.

## Funeral or Memorial Service Details

**What date, time and place is the funeral or memorial service taking place?**

Date:

Time:

Location:

**Who is the celebrant or minister leading the service?**

Name:

Telephone Number:

Email:

**At what point in the order of service will you speak?**

Answer:

*My suggestion, if you have a choice, is to speak as soon as possible in the service, so you are not waiting for a long time. It not only adds to your understandable anxiety, but you will miss what others are saying before you, your mind preoccupied with saying your words. So ask the person leading if you can speak early in the service.*

**How long will you want/be allowed to speak?**

Answer:

*Have they have given you a time limit? In step two, there is a word calculator to help you know how much to write for the time you have. My recommendation from experience is to aim for 7 - 8 minutes of speaking time. You will find more information about this later on. It may sound a long time, but don't worry, everything you will need to do that is here in this toolkit.*

**Who else will speak at the funeral or memorial service?**

Additional Speakers:

*You may need to ask the celebrant or minister about this. It helps for to know so you don't say the same things.*

**Are there specific people you would like to thank in your words?**

I want to say thank you to:

*It's important to thank those people who have helped you or your loved one. This may be family and friends who can't be at the service because of illness or distance. It may be carers, nurses, doctors or perhaps neighbours who have been there for the person. This is an important simple act of kindness to others on the day and will mean so much to them.*

**Will there be a live stream or online video feed for the service?**

Is there a live webcast or an online funeral video link? Yes/No

Who do you know will watch who you want to thank?

*This is useful information to know as you may want to thank those people watching from around the world. It makes them feel part of the service rather than only watching from a distance. When I take a service with a webcast, I will look up to camera usually at the back of the room. I welcome those who are watching. If you know someone by name, thank them personally. It will be special for them feeling like an observer, and also for them people in attendance as much.*

## Biographical Information

*Why might you need these details? It is more common to tell the biographical details of a person in an obituary. For example, their place of birth, parents, and siblings, schooling, career, etc. But you may need to reference something in your few words.*

### What is their full name?

Name:

*Were they known by any other names? Was there an affectionate nickname or term of endearment you used to call each other? What name feels best to use in your words of eulogy? Which will be the name you will use most in the words you say?*

### What is their date of birth?

Date: — / — / —

### Where were they born?

Place:

### What were their parent's names?

Father: _____

Mother: _____

### Did they have any brothers or sisters? Were they older or younger?

Siblings in age order:

# Chapter 5

## DISCOVERING CHARACTER TRAITS AND PERSONALITY THEMES

'I think a lot of what we learn about others isn't what they tell us. It's what we observe.'

Iain Reid

WRITING A FEW WORDS and making them relevant, personal and memorable begins by identifying the person's key personality themes and character traits.

What is it that makes them – them?

Getting these traits listed, then identifying the key ones, builds the solid foundation you will use to say your few words.

This worksheet helps you find those themes and traits which are the essence of the person. You may also uncover one overriding theme of their life. This could be useful as a theme for your words, too. I will explain more about that later.

What are those things which make us an individual unique and distinctive from everyone else?

- They can be our life roles as a being a spouse, parent, brother or sister or friend.

- They can be our career choices as being an engineer, shop manager, academic or homemaker or retired.

- They can be our place of birth, language, or accent. The sound of our laughter, or the way we dress.

- They can be our love of animals, being a gifted musician, raving sports fan or a volunteer for a charity.

Behind all of those life roles, hobbies and interests is the essence of who we are. Those key things that make us – us.

Those are our unique personality themes and character traits.

We all have personality themes and character traits. However, it is a one-off combination of those that makes us the unique and recognisable person we are. It is what makes us the complex, multifaceted person everyone knows and loves.

In this worksheet, we will identify your loved one's key personality themes and character traits. There are no right or wrong answers here. Some will be more instantly recognisable and prominent, others will be clear on reflection.

**Discovering An Overriding Life Theme.**

In thinking about your loved one's personality themes and character traits, you may also discover an **overriding life theme** could emerge. You may find you keep coming back to the same thoughts to describe them.

For example, descriptive words such as unselfish, serving, kind and loving seem to capture and define everything they did. It is as if the person lived their life for the love of others.

It may be, when talking to family and friends, it's the same words and themes which are used by them too. Look out for it. This is helpful, and a significant point for you to notice in writing the few words you will say. It resonates with those listening to your words if you have an overriding life theme.

It could be someone who faced many challenging periods in their life. Perhaps they fought with courage through an illness or served their country with bravery. It made them a person of commitment, someone determined, stoic and resilient. You could describe them as an overcomer, even a hero of sorts.

Maybe whenever you were around the person, they were smiling, optimistic, the glass of their life overflowing to everyone around them. Their overriding life theme was bringing sunshine and positivity into the lives of others. Maybe it was empathy that was the defining theme of their life?

Or, it may even be the theme of their life they were stubborn and single-minded. It's no surprise often played at funerals is 'My Way' by Frank Sinatra.

The research and words you will say are not the place to make a judgement about the personality themes and character traits they had, but to identify them.

An overriding life theme often serves as the title and theme for the eulogies I write. By adding an appropriate and carefully researched quote it makes the words memorable.

The printed order of service brochures common at funerals and memorials often includes the words, 'A Eulogy - or A Tribute.' People attending keep these sheets as a remembrance. The words quickly slip away from memory after being said on the day. Yet, if you have a title linked to the person's personality themes and character traits, it brings those words back to mind many years later.

In the Common Questions & Bonus Worksheets section, you will find - **Bonus Worksheet 3 – 10 Overriding Life Themes.**

These are ten overriding life themes, titles and accompanying quotations I've used in eulogies. Use them for inspiration or incorporate them into your words of eulogy for your loved one.

**Overriding Life Theme Titles**

- You Could Never Take That Unceasing Shine Away
- A Friend Who Held Life Together
- Greater Than Riches
- It's What We Do That Matters
- Beautiful People Don't Just Happen
- Love Endures
- Always There
- Comprehending The Mystery Every Day
- The Quiet Hero
- What A Ride!

Remember, it is impossible to say everything you could say about the person on the day. But if through your words you highlight those key personality themes and character traits others feel and have observed about the person, it will make your words sound relevant, personal, and memorable. It helps others feel and say, 'Yes, that's the person I remember as well.'

# Chapter 6

# Worksheet 2 - Discovering Personality Themes and Character Traits

## How To Complete Worksheet 2 – Discovering Personality Themes & Character Traits

**First:** HIGHLIGHT ALL THOSE personality themes and character traits most instantly recognisable. Add any missing ones which could describe the person you know.

**Second:** narrow that list down to identify the **top ten**.

**Third:** from the list of ten, identify the **top three** personality themes and character traits.

These will become the **three key themes - A, B, C** of your eulogy words. It will be from these three key personality themes and character traits you draw stories, memories and thoughts to shape into the few words for your eulogy.

List the top ten primary personality themes and character traits.

1.

2.

3.

4.

5.

6.

7.

8.

9.

10.

Chose three from the above list as the final three key personality themes and character traits we will use in your words.

**Key Theme A** _____

**Key Theme B** _____

**Key Theme C** _____

Have you discovered an overriding theme of their life?

Try to sum it up in one word or a short sentence.

**The overriding theme of their life could be:**

Remember, review the Bonus Worksheet 3 – 10 Overriding Life Theme Eulogy Titles & Quotations at the back of the workbook.

# Personality Themes and Character Traits

| | | |
|---|---|---|
| Adventurous | Good-natured | Practical |
| Ambitious | Happy | Principled |
| Competitive | Hardworking | Protective |
| Caring | Helpful | Reliable |
| Charismatic | Heroic | Respectful |
| Compassionate | Humble | Selfless |
| Conscientious | Insightful | Sentimental |
| Considerate | Intelligent | Sociable |
| Courageous | Kind | Spontaneous |
| Creative | Logical | Sporting |
| Curious | Lovable | Stoic |
| Determined | Loyal | Sympathetic |
| Decisive | Maternal | Stubborn |
| Dedicated | Meticulous | Stylish |
| Dignified | Optimistic | Tolerant |
| Enthusiastic | Organised | Understanding |
| Fair | Patient | Unchanging |
| Friendly | Perceptive | Warm |
| Fun-loving | Persuasive | Wise |
| Generous | Playful | Witty |
| Gentle | Placid | Welcoming |

# Chapter 7

## WHAT FOUR KEY QUESTIONS REKINDLE EMOTIONAL MEMORIES?

'How we spend our days is, of course, how we spend our lives.'

Annie Dillard

IN THIS SECTION, YOU will build on your research by asking four key questions about your loved one. I designed each of these questions as a writing prompt about memories of emotions and feelings.

I design these questions to recall the values and even quirky ways of the person. To reflect on how much and in what ways they affected your life.

We will come back to the answers you write in step two when we draft your words into stories. For now, try to answer the questions as best you can.

Remember, we may not use all this information, but in taking time to think through the answers to these questions, it will prompt beautiful memories of your loved one. Use the note pages as the back of the workbook for memories, thoughts, and stories that come to mind.

# Chapter 8

# Worksheet 3 - Four Key Questions

## 1: How did they make you feel?

FOR EXAMPLE:

- Unconditionally loved and cared for.
- Inspired and encouraged.
- Never judged or criticised, only accepted.
- Always happy.
- Seen and heard.
- They made me smile.

**Being with my loved one made me feel...**

List your feelings:

Now you try bringing these words and phrases into a sentence to express how they made you feel.

Here are some examples:

They were **patient** and made me feel at ease. Because of this, their **calm ways** allowed me to express myself without fear of judgment.

They were **honest** and made me feel secure. Because of this, their **transparency and integrity** built a foundation of trust and reliability in our relationship.

They were **loyal**, and it made me feel supported. Because of this, their **commitment and unwavering devotion** made me feel confident that I could rely on them through thick and thin.

Now you try using this same formula to express how they made you feel in a few sentences.

**They were:**




**And it made me feel:**




**Because of this their:**

## 2: What were the key values and priorities in their life?

For example:

For them, family always came first, providing for our needs and wants. Duty, honesty, integrity and justice in all dealings. Maybe determination in overcoming problems and living with optimism.

**The key values of their life were:**

## 3: What was the best advice about life they gave you?

For example:

Always live respecting others, especially your elders. Being polite, punctual and keeping your word. Never giving up, no matter how hard life gets. How to enjoy life by being content. Self-confidence, self-assurance, or a spirit of adventure. They had an understanding of what a good parent or kind person is like.

Now you.

**The best advice about life they gave me was:**

## 4: How do you think they would like to be remembered?

For example:

Someone who wasn't perfect but tried to live the best life they could. A loving, loyal, and unselfish person. A person committed to their family and community and made the world a little better by the way they lived.

**I think the way they would like to be remembered is:**

# Chapter 9

## IMAGINING THEIR PERFECT DAY

'A perfect day is when the sun is shining, the breeze is blowing, the birds are singing, and the lawn mower is broken.'

James Dent

LIFE COMPRISES WORK, CHORES, and commitments. In between, we can have time to choose. Choose to rest, relax and pass the time doing those things we enjoy, activities to grow our minds, exercise our bodies and feed our souls.

One way I have found to build a picture of how someone enjoyed their 'one wild and precious life' is to ask, 'How would they have spent their perfect day?' What would a perfect day look like?

'But I do not know how they would spend a perfect day?' You may be thinking.

Here, take a few moments, close your eyes, and let your recollections and imagination blend. By taking time to think like this, often you can find stories, memories and ideas for things you can say.

Thinking about their perfect day brings to mind the joy, happiness and fun the person enjoyed about life. We can forget those amid our sadness, not remembering those times when life was special and happy for them, and that's a good way to think about someone we have lost. Bringing some of these thoughts and memories into your words will remind those listening how much they enjoyed the days of their life as well.

# Chapter 10

# WORKSHEET 4 – PERFECT DAY PLANNER

## Perfect Day Planner

- How would the perfect day begin?

- Where would they be?

- What fun things would they do?

- Would they be watching their favourite sports team, cheering them on winning or losing?

- What about being snuggled up on the sofa, the latest binge worthy Netflix series cued up, and enough chocolate to open a sweet store?

- Playing the latest PlayStation game for hours?

- Seeing unknown places, embracing different cultures, tasting alternative cuisines?

- Would it be tending the soil, hands deep in the earth, cultivating a garden?

- How about on a riverbank, watching for the telltale sign a fish is about to take the bait under the float?

- Would you find them in a quiet corner snuggled up on a cosy chair engrossed in a book by their favourite writer?

- Or visiting a favourite restaurant, or watching the TV with a takeaway on their lap?

**A perfect day would be:**

# Takeaways & Actions from Step One: Research

## Important Takeaways:

- Eulogy writing starts with research - collecting thoughts, memories, and feelings about your loved one.

- Try to recall the specific details that make your memories personal.

- Completing the four research worksheets helps you recall memories.

- You may discover an overriding life theme that defines your loved one, for example, themes such as kindness, resilience, or optimism.

- Involving others in the research process can help gather more memories and stories. (See Bonus Worksheet 6 for an email to send.)

- Don't expect your words to include everything about the person, only the key themes and traits that made them unique. Use the note pages as the back of the workbook for memories, thoughts, and stories that come to mind.

## Action Points:

1. Start filling in the Basic Information for the funeral or memorial service.

2. Identify the person's key personality themes and character traits. Narrow down to the top three that define them the most.

3. Answer four key questions about how the person made you feel, their values, their impact on your life, and how you think they'd like to be remembered.

4. Fill in Worksheet 4, The Perfect Day Planner, to help build a picture of how your loved one enjoyed their life.

5. Reach out to others if you need for their memories and stories to add depth to your research.

6. Be patient with yourself and take breaks when needed.

7. If you need more inspiration or help, refer to the **Common Questions & Bonus Resources section**

# STEP TWO: DRAFT

# Chapter 11

## FROM MEMORIES TO MANUSCRIPT: HOW TO START DRAFTING YOUR EULOGY

WELL DONE ON COMPLETING step one. Next, we will take the research you have completed and write the first draft of your eulogy.

In this section, we will cover these topics:

- Why a simple structure helps guide your writing.

- How to write the three middle sections of your eulogy as mini-stories.

- Why we apply the use of transitions between sections.

- How to write a conclusion.

- How to write an introduction.

By now, completing the worksheets, you will have collected many memories, stories, and thoughts about your loved one. Through the smiles, laughter, tears and mixed emotions, it is perhaps the first time you have thought about them so much in a short space of time. There will be so many ideas of what you could say in the few words of eulogy you will write.

Let's begin now to take those memories and shape them into your words you will say. We do this by writing a **First Draft.**

Here's something to remember as you start—you cannot say everything you will want to say in the time you have. It's always a challenge. Every eulogy I write feels like there could be so much more to say. You will feel the same. Writing a first draft helps you decide what to include in your words.

**Here is an important fact about writing your first draft.**

The trick of writing a first draft of your words is not **writing** and **editing** at the same time.

**Writing** is getting the stories, memories and words from your research down on paper or on a computer.

**Editing** is shaping those into the words into what you will say on the day.

It takes a distinct part of our brain to get the stories and memories into words. But it is a different part of our reasoning we use to edit the words.

People say about themselves, 'I'm not a writer. I can't spell, my grammar is rubbish. I don't know the difference between a comma, or colon.'

Let me let you in on a well-kept secret.

**It doesn't matter!**

It's a hidden secret – you might think authors, and speechwriters pick up a pen or open a word processing document and the words and sentences flow in perfect prose, with no spelling errors or missing full stops.

NO! That's not what happens.

Every first draft is a messy draft. Every first scribble needs shaping and refining. Then those words are often edited by someone paid to edit them.

So don't get hung up on writing perfect sentences at this stage. Don't worry if you start thinking, 'This is not good, it doesn't sound right.' Let me reassure you, it always feels that way when you are writing.

Here are a few more helpful tips to remember you when you write your first draft.

- Get your first words written. A first draft is not a final version. It is a starting point for more work. The first draft is messy, a sketch, an outline that gets you going.

- Write. Don't worry about sentence structure, spelling, grammar or how it will sound; simply write at this stage. Using short words, sentences and brief paragraphs is better than longer.

- We all have an 'inner critic.' The voice in our heads telling us the words we are writing are rubbish. Nobody will think they are anything like the person we are talking about, and so on. Silence your 'inner critic' by writing.

- Don't try to write it all in one go. You will start with the key themes A, B and C, you listed in the worksheets. Then work on your conclusion and introduction. It's easier to write these sections when you know the three key themes you will use.

- Take each section one step at a time. Review the research you have collected and add as much specific detail as you can. You find that as you focus your mind on each key theme, more memories will come back to you. It doesn't matter how randomly the memories come.

- Write what comes to mind. Use the note pages as the back of the workbook for additional memories, thoughts, and stories that come to mind.

- Use a computer or the worksheets, whatever works best for you. The important thing is bringing the ideas together. You can edit and polish the words in the next section when you edit.

Let me encourage you to keep moving forward, step by step.

You may be feeling overwhelmed now, or worried about how everything will come together. It will. If you can write one rough sentence that captures the essence of what you want to say about the person, you're on your way to writing a short eulogy of memorable few words. Only take the next step.

We are going to create the first draft of your words using a simple outline for your words. Let me explain a little more about what that is and why it will help you.

# Chapter 12

# WHY USE THIS SIMPLE EULOGY OUTLINE?

## Why Does Using A Simple Eulogy Outline Help?

SAYING A FEW WORDS that are memorable, relevant, and personal is much easier when you use an outline. An outline guides you in writing the words of your first draft and helps you speak in a planned and prepared way. Having a simple outline to follow makes your words flow logically. This helps those people listening stay interested and, most importantly, makes your words more memorable.

**What Is The Best Way To Outline Your Words?**

This is a question I am often asked, and my suggestion after writing and hearing hundreds of eulogies is this: keep it simple.

Here is the simple outline you will use for your words.

You start with an **Introduction.**

Then you have three **Middle Sections.**

**Section 1 –**

**Section 2 –**

**Section 3 –**

You finish with a **Conclusion.**

**Let's look at this simple eulogy speech outline in more detail.**

**1 – Introduction**

What do you include in your introduction?

The opening sentences in your introduction are going to paint a word picture of the person to capture an essence of who they were. We want to grab and keep the attention of everyone there. It's important to highlight their personality and characteristics as soon as you start. You want everyone there to say, 'Yes, that's the person I remember too.' If you want to use an overriding life theme, this is where you should introduce it.

Depending on who else might speak at the funeral or memorial service, it may be necessary to add some of the biographical details you collected in Worksheet 1 – Basic Information. It is better to limit these to a minimum for a couple of reasons.

First, it uses the limited time you have listing a series of facts (they were born here, went to school there, etc).

Second, it takes time away from talking about who the person was to you, and everyone there, rather than what they did for work, etc. It's those personal and specific memories, stories and feelings that will make your words memorable.

In **Worksheet 9 – Writing The Introduction** - you will find simple steps to follow that will help you write your introduction

## 2. Middle Three Sections

Next, in each of the three middle sections, we will highlight one of the key themes you have identified in the research section. Using short stories, specific memories and feelings, we then expand on that one key personality theme.

2 – **Section 1** – (The words you will say come from Key Theme A)

In this section, we will highlight what made them unique and special. How this key theme was clear in their life using stories and specific examples.

3 – **Section 2** – (The words you will say come from Key Theme B)

In this section, again using notes from your research on this theme, we will add more specific details and perhaps you could add a memorable experience you shared.

4 – **Section 3** – (The words you will say come Key Theme C)

As well as bringing to mind why this theme was important in their life, we will add what you learned from them and how your life is different and richer because of them.

5 – **Conclusion**

What do you include in your conclusion?

Your conclusion is where you remind everyone of those key themes which made the person unique and special. It is where you will leave a lasting thought of the legacy they leave behind and say a last farewell.

In **Worksheet 8 – Writing The Conclusion** — you will find the steps you need to write your conclusion.

**Why use this simple speech outline?**

There is an adage about public speaking which goes something like:

- Tell them what you're going to tell them.
- Tell them.
- Tell them what you've told them.

It is the simplest and most effective way of structuring a speech. It's been around for centuries. Why? Your introduction should capture people's attention. Each of the middle sections expands on those three key personality traits and character traits. Your conclusion brings everything together. Reminding people of what you have said and help you say your last farewell.

# Chapter 13

# How Many Words Will You Need To Write?

It helps at this stage to know the number of words you will need for the eulogy. For most people, aiming to speak for about 7-8 minutes is a good starting point.

So thinking back to the simple outline here is your plan for speaking 7-8 minutes.

Introduction – (120-200 words) = 10%

Section 1 – (200-250 words)

Section 2 – (200-250 words) = 80%

Section 3 – (200-250 words)

Conclusion – (120-200 words) = 10%

In total, somewhere around 1000 - 12000 words or about one and a half to two A4 pages in size 12 font, single spaced.

Using the words-for-time information above, if you wanted to speak for longer, you could either extend each of the three middle sections with more words. Another option would be to add further sections by using some of the other personality themes and character traits you identified.

Work on needing around 115 -130 words for every minute you want to speak.

In the **Common Questions & Bonus Worksheets** section at the back of this toolkit, you will find:

- **Bonus worksheet 1** – The Lifeline Exercise

- **Bonus worksheet 2** – Life Lessons and Legacy

- **Bonus worksheet 3** – 10 Overriding Life Themes

- **Bonus worksheet 4** – 36 Extra Memory Prompt Questions

- **Bonus Worksheet 5** – 26 Quotations For Telling A Life Story

These will help you find even more information to add to your words if you need them.

Now, let's begin by writing your first draft. You will start by writing your three middle sections. Then a conclusion. Finally, the introduction.

# Chapter 14

# TURNING YOUR MEMORIES INTO MINI-STORIES

'Kind words can be short and easy to speak, but their echoes are truly endless.'
Mother Teresa

## How Do I Write The Three Middle Sections Turning Them Into Mini-Stories?

By now, you will have three key personality themes and character traits you have identified from Worksheet 2, and maybe an overriding life theme you are going to use.

It's worth saying again: there could be so many things you could say, so many stories to tell. Hopefully, it's from these three key sections most people will identify with your words.

There will always be more to say.

But by identifying those stories, you could write them down and store them away in a memory journal for the future. Use the note pages as the back of the workbook for memories, thoughts, and stories that come to mind.

This could be something precious to keep for the future, or to share with others.

But for now, we will only concentrate on the three middle sections of your writing. There are many examples for you to see and follow in this section.

### Writing The Three Middle Sections Into Mini-Stories

Here is something important to notice right at the start of drafting these three middle sections. Try to remember and use specifics if you can. So often we speak in general terms, but we experience things specifically.

Bringing those particular and specific memories to mind is what we will do for our three middle sections.

### Kipling's Six Serving Men Writing Formula

When writing, to help you think in specifics, keep in mind Rudyard Kipling's 'Six serving men.'

> I keep six honest serving-men
> (They taught me all I knew);
> Their names are What and Why and When
> And How and Where and Who.
>
> Rudyard Kipling

**Kipling's Writing Formula For Memories**

**What** – is the precise memory?

**Why** – is this important or special?

**When** – locate the memory in the exact time if you can.

**How** – did the special memory happen?

**Where** – locate the memory in its exact place.

**Who** – was it you alone? Who else was in the memory?

It could be a sentence. Maybe it will stretch to a paragraph or two, or even a couple of pages. At this stage, we are simply writing the memories and exploring our shared experiences with this person, recalling stories that evoke laughter, smiles, tears, or a combination of emotions.

At the top of the worksheets that follow, write in the space provided the Key Theme - **A, B or C** you identified and then write as many things as you can about the way they acted and lived in that way.

You often find one memory leads to another memory, idea to idea. Go back over your notes in the research sections. Write as much as you can without stopping to think too much. Remember, at this stage, we are collecting those specific memories.

Next, you will turn those ideas and memories into a paragraph like a mini-story.

## Turning Your Ideas and Memories Into A Mini-Story

What we mean here by mini-story is to write a few sentences, a couple of paragraphs, to expand a little of the three key themes you have chosen. Each mini-story will be around 250-300 words long.

When you think about it, often our favourite stories start with, 'Once upon a time.' 'As soon as you hear that phrase, you know a story is coming. It pricks our attention, and we listen in closer. That is what you want to do with the beginning of each of your three middle sections.

Begin your middle sections by using some of Kipling's writing formula. By using these prompts, you can streamline your words and tell the story.

For example, let's consider your loved one. When you listed the personality themes and character traits, let's say the first of your three middle themes is kindness. One dictionary definition of kindness is 'the quality of being friendly, generous, and considerate.'

When you say in your words, they were 'kind', we all understand what we mean, when it is we experience receiving kindness. When we add a specific, as in where something happened and what happened, it resonates with everyone at the service deeper. It's more focused. It's personal and, above all, memorable.

Let's look at some examples of if it was a father you were writing about. Thinking back, and looking over your research, you remember how your dad would always be there for you as a 'free taxi' service as a teenager. Let's use this as an example.

**When** did it happen?

*When I was 16, at home, as I was finding my feet in life. I was excited about a night out, but at the same time, a bit unsure.*

**Where** was a time they expressed kindness to you?

*It was one of the first nights I wanted to go out with my friends to a party. Their parents would not be there. It was not dad's favourite idea! But he had patience and understanding.*

**What** was it they did?

*No matter what time of night or where it was, dad said he would wait. He promised me he would be around the corner and if I was not happy, I could leave and he would be there.*

**How** did their kindness to you make you feel?

*Knowing he was there, I felt safe and protected. As I got older, he would always be there to collect me, no matter how late or where I would be.*

## Examples of A Mini-Story

### Dad's Free Taxi Service

*I was 16. There was a 'no parents allowed' party. It was the first time I was allowed out later than a normal curfew of 10:00 p.m. Coming home times were never negotiable in our house. I was excited,*

*I was also anxious. Anxious in the way teenagers are. Dad, well, he was anxious in the way dads are with teenage girls aged 16 going to their first 'no parents allowed party!'*

*Dad was kind in everything he did. Kindness was at the core of his soul. Sitting me down, he read me the riot act. Warned me about spiked drinks, and then a 'what boys are thinking' talk... (oh dad, it was so embarrassing.) That night, he waited. Just in case I wanted to come home. I didn't. But he still waited for me until past midnight.*

*As I got older, no matter what time I needed him to collect me from a party or night out, like a free taxi, dad was always there! If I kept him waiting, he never complained. He never tutted or made it feel like a chore. Even if I couldn't say too much in the car, being tired from dancing all night.*

*I never felt worried or uncertain, but always safe in the front passenger seat of the old blue Ford Fiesta next to him. We'd travel home listening to Frank Sinatra singing 'Fly Me To The Moon' on the cassette player. Dad's active kindness in my life has always made me feel safe, secure, and unconditionally loved.*

**Note** – the above 'mini-story' is 257 words. This is the about the length of each middle section you need to write.

For another couple of examples, say one of the overriding themes was dad's **generosity**. In what way?

As with kindness, we understand the general term, but it's the **specific** we are looking for.

Was it generosity with time or money, or possessions? Was it being willing to listen, being generous with attention? Or generous with influence, guiding your life?

*I knew that whenever I needed help, Dad would be there. I always knew dad was never too busy for me. He was always on the end of the phone. 'How do I put petrol in the car?' 'Do I need oil every week?' He never judged me, never made me feel anything less than unconditionally loved. 'No problem,' he'd say. 'I'll be around in ten minutes and help.' And he was.*

Or:

*Mum was innately maternal. It was in her very soul to care for us. Her magic kisses on cuts, endless bedtime stories, tasty raspberry jam, Victoria sponge cakes and clean school clothes waiting at the end of the bed every day. She never stopped caring for us.*

*I can see now how she never had time for herself, but I don't think that mattered to her. We were her world, my brother and sisters and I. She would have given us her last breath. It inspires me to be a mum like that to Maisie and George, her grandchildren. She inspires me every day to be the best mum I can be.*

If we can add a feeling (How) as well, that's even more impactful. Don't forget to remember to use all your senses in your memories. What smells, for instance, could link to kindness or generosity?

Look back over your answers in **Worksheet 3 – Four Key Questions**. There you will have listed some feelings. Ask yourself, what did they **do** to make me **feel** that way? What specific action did they take?

## How To You Move from A to B and B to C In The Middle Sections Using Transitions?

Before you start, there is one other thing important for the three middle sections to mention: transitions.

As you move from Key Theme A to Key Theme B, and Key Theme B to Key Theme C, each time you will add a simple link phrase, or a transition between helping your words flow.

Transitions are like a signpost to tell the people listening where you are going next. It helps you guide them to the next memory you want to recall, and it helps them keep in mind what you have remembered about the person.

They are a simple phrase to add to move your words forward.

Here are a few simple transitions you could use:

- Although I know you all remember dad's kindness, in the same way you will all remember his sense of humour…

- So as well as being kind, dad was also a generous man…

- Besides being generous, dad was loyal…

- Now I've mentioned how mum was… let me mention coupled to this how she was…

- But that's not the only thing you will remember…

- Last, but similarly important to remember is…

Try to use a different transition to get from theme A to theme B to theme C.

We have covered a lot in this section.

Now it's your turn to start writing a first draft. We will start with **Worksheet 5 – Key personality theme A.**

# Chapter 15

## Worksheet 5 – Memory 1 – Key Theme A

In this worksheet, you need to focus all your thoughts and memories on **Key Theme A**.

### Take Key Theme A and enter it here:

Here are some questions to consider as you think about the person and that theme.

Think of a specific memory from the past (*like dad's free taxi service*).

What – are the specifics of the memory? Sights, sounds, smells, feelings?

Why – is this theme important or special to you and others? How did it make you feel?

When – can you locate the memories in an exact time?

How – did the special memory happen?

Where – can you locate and memories in their exact place?

Who – was it you and the person alone? Who else was in the memory?

What is your lasting memory of how this theme was in their life?

What is it about this theme that makes you laugh, cry, be grateful, or want to copy in your life?

# Key Theme A Notes:

# Chapter 16

## Worksheet 6 – Memory 2 – Key Theme B

IN THIS WORKSHEET, YOU need to focus all your thoughts and memories on **Key Theme B**.

### Take Key Theme B and enter it here:

Here are some questions to consider as you think about the person and that theme.

How did this key theme show itself in their life?

What is your lasting memory of how this theme was clear?

What did you learn from them or about life from this theme?

What is it about this theme that makes you laugh, cry, be grateful, or want to copy in your life?

What – are the specifics of the memory? Sights, sounds, smells, feelings?

Why – is this theme important or special to you and others? How did it make you feel?

When – can you locate the memories in an exact time?

How – did the special memory happen?

Where – can you locate and memories in their exact place?

Who – was it you and the person alone? Who else was in the memory?

**Key Theme B Notes:**

# Chapter 17

## WORKSHEET 7 – MEMORY 3 – KEY THEME C

IN THIS WORKSHEET, YOU need to focus all your thoughts and memories on **Key Theme C**.

### Take Key Theme C and enter it here:

Here are some questions to consider as you think about the person and that theme.

How did this key theme show itself in their life?

What is your lasting memory of how this theme was clear?

What did you learn from them or about life from this theme?

What is it about this theme that makes you laugh, cry, be grateful, or want to copy in your life?

What – are the specifics of the memory? Sights, sounds, smells, feelings?

Why – is this theme important or special to you and others? How did it make you feel?

When – can you locate the memories in an exact time?

How – did the special memory happen?

Where – can you locate and memories in their exact place?

Who – was it you and the person alone? Who else was in the memory?

**Key Theme C Notes:**

# Chapter 18

# How To Write The Conclusion

How do you write a conclusion that leaves a lasting memory of your loved one?

Often eulogy speeches end or fall apart with a throwaway line.

'I'm glad that's over.'
'OK, I'm finished.'
'I think that is all I want to say.'

It is understandable, because it is how you will feel when you get to the end of your words.

Not thinking about and planning your last words takes away so much from all what you have worked hard to bring together. It robs your words of significance and the importance of the memories you have recalled.

**Having a strong conclusion to your words is important for many reasons.**

**1 - It signals you are ending the words you want to say.**

By giving those listening a sign you are coming towards the end of your few words, it creates attention and focus on what you are saying. When you stop speaking at the end of a speech without warning, it leaves people confused and feeling that something is missing.

**2 - What we remember most is what we hear first and last.**

In psychology, and public speaking, this has a name – the **primacy effect** and the **recency effect**.

The **primacy effect** is what you say in your introduction, how you start your words. The **recency effect** is what you say at the end. People will remember what you say at the end of your words.

A strong conclusion gives you the opportunity to remind those listening of how special the person was to you. In your conclusion, you will point to those three key themes and overriding life theme again. The recency effect will help those words stay in the minds of the people listening as you finish and sit down. Then and as they leave the service, those words will echo long afterwards.

In your conclusion, we bring all these thoughts together and add what will be your lasting memories, and their legacy, as time goes forward. As we will do in your introduction, we have a simple step-by-step process to help write your conclusion.

## Four Steps For Crafting A Memorable Conclusion

1. **Signal** that you are coming to the end of your words.

2. **Remind people** of the three key personality themes and character traits, and also the overriding life theme, if you have used one.

3. Share **a lasting final thought** about your loved one.

4. Finish with **an uplifting sentence.**

Let's expand further on each of these steps.

Step 1: **Signal that you are coming to the end of your words.**

First, use a phrase or signal to show that you are coming to the end of your words. This raises attention and tells people you are about to bring your words to a close. There are many ways to do this. Here are a few ideas you could use.

**You could say:**

- *'As I close these few words today...'*

- *'There are so many more things I could say today, but finally...'*

- *'The last thoughts I want to leave with you are...'*

**You could ask a rhetorical question:**

- *'What will you remember most about my dad?'*

- *'To finish, if you could only say one thing about my mom, what would it be?'*

- *'How can I ever express everything I would like to say today about my loved one? I can't. But in closing...'*

**You could use a quotation or a catchphrase they used:**

- *'Dad never said 'Goodbye' when we parted, but always, 'Stay safe, sweetheart.' As I finish, I'm going to do the same. It's not goodbye, dad; it's stay safe.'*

- *'As I began these words today, I used the quote by Walt Whitman, 'Some people are so much sunshine to the square inch.' As I finish these words, let me return to that, because that's how I will always remember mom.'*

- *'Let me close with the words of Henry Fielding, a writer, 'I am content; that is a blessing greater than riches; and he to whom that is given need ask no more.' On that basis, my dad was probably the richest person you knew. He was content with his life.'*

**Step two in your conclusion is to:**

**Remind people** of the three key personality themes and character traits, and also the overriding life theme, if you have used one.

You remind those listening of the three key personality themes and character traits in the same order as you presented them.

Now is not the place to anything new, or to tell another story, though you will feel there is always more you could have said.

Reminding people in your conclusion helps them remember these three key themes better. It's repetition that makes these words memorable. Please notice, depending on what they were, you might need a shift in tense (this is what I will speak about – in your introduction) to the past tense (this is what I have spoken about in the conclusion).

- *'While overall it was dad's confidence that marked his life, I will never forget dad's kindness, generosity and humour.'*

- *'When I think of mom, it will be always be how understanding, supporting and loving she was.'*

- *'Not a day will pass when I don't remember how dad would never give up on you, never abandon you, and never stop fighting for you.'*

**The third step in your conclusion is to:**

Share a **lasting final thought** about your loved one.

You could end with a sentence that has something of personal meaning for you, or to say how you will go forward from here.

- *'He was the best dad I could ever have had.'*

- *'Everything good and right about being a mom myself, I learned from my mom.'*

- *'I wouldn't have wanted anyone else by side through those years.'*

**The fourth and final step in your conclusion is to:**

Finish with an **uplifting sentence.**

To finish saying your few words, it's good to use an uplifting sentence. It brings what you have said to a positive conclusion. It's a moment to inspire those there to live their days the way the person lived, or to act in a certain way they did, both of which reinforce their legacy.

You can do this by:

- Asking a rhetorical question.

- Encouraging a call to take an action.

- Inspiring those listening to visualise their future life.


The impact of your words can give those there a moment to reflect on how special but how fragile life can be. To reconsider the effects of their actions, in the light of how someone else lived, and to embrace their finite humanity. We each have one life to live, and what will be the total of that life?

**You could say:**

- *'What can we learn from dad's life? How better would life be for everyone if we all lived with his kindness, generosity and humour each day? I'll try to live like dad every day. I'm going to do my best to live his way each day. What about you?'*

- *'I've learned from mom's life to see those around me who need help, who need someone to take action. We can make the same impact in our life as she did, if we understand, support and love the lost and lonely as she did. The question is, I suppose, will we? It's my determination in her memory to do so in my life.'*

- *'We each have a chance to make a little difference in our life to the world around us. It's those little acts of kindness dad did at every opportunity that made my life, and those who knew him beautiful. How different would the world be if we all did that by his example? That is such a wonderful legacy to leave by his life well lived.'*


Then, with these last words spoken, take a moment to pause, scan all those listening with gentle eye contact, and say, 'Thank you.' Then return to your seat.

# Chapter 19

# Worksheet 8 - Writing The Conclusion

**Worksheet 8 - Writing The Conclusion**

Now complete the sections in this worksheet to write a draft of your conclusion.

**Signal that you are coming to the end of your words.**

**Remind people of the three key personality themes and character traits and also the overriding life theme, if you have used one.**

**Share a lasting final thought about your loved one.**

**Finish with an uplifting sentence.**

# Chapter 20

## How To Write The Introduction

> I've learned that people will forget what you said, people will forget what you did, but people will never forget how you made them feel.
>
> Maya Angelou

IT MIGHT SEEM STRANGE, but writing your introduction is much easier at the end than at the beginning. So that is why we have left it to end!

Remember, and this is important. What you will say in your opening and closing words is what people will remember most about the your loved one.

**Avoiding More Throwaway Lines**

Because of nerves, or even perhaps not knowing what to say, often people open a few words of any speech as they end them with what I call a throwaway line.

- 'I'm not used to speaking in public, but wanted to say some words today.'
- 'Can you hear me at the back?'
- 'Where shall I start?'
- 'We are here to talk about dad's life.' (Everyone knows that, so why say it?)

By doing this, you take away all the attention from the person you want to speak about. It detracts from the moment of significance and fails to capture people's attention. Once you lose attention, it's hard, almost impossible, to get it back.

**Focusing On Your Loved One**

But if you open the words you want to say by focusing on the person, it makes a world of difference in three key ways.

- It instantly captures people's attention.

- It helps them immediately picture in their mind your loved one or friend.

- It makes those there want to hear more of what you will say.

This is the purpose of your few words: to evoke thoughts and feelings about your loved one who has passed away. Not to have any focus on you, the speaker, or the audience who is listening.

Focusing on the person first brings to mind memories and feelings for everyone listening. It makes them say in their minds, 'Yes, that's how I remember them, too.'

Here's a key thing: knowing your opening words well will help you too.

It's only natural you will be nervous when you speak. That's normal for everyone who speaks in public. Saying these few words will be a challenge for you, as it is for anyone trying to deliver a eulogy. But knowing the exact words that you will say in the first few seconds, in the opening sentences, gives you confidence to start. It will allow you to even relax a little so everyone can hear what you are saying and resonate with your memories.

Let's look at how to write your introduction.

## How Do You Write An Engaging Introduction?

Open with the **Rule of Three**.

**Point forward** to the **Three Key Themes** identified in the **Personality Themes and Character Traits** you will talk about later.

**Introduce** yourself.

Say **thank you**.

In the worksheet that follows, you can fill in the sections for this outline formula when you write your own words. But for now, let me briefly explain why this outline for an introduction will help you.

### Step 1. Open With The Rule of Three

This introduction formula uses The Rule of Three.

The Rule of Three is a common way of presenting ideas in a speech.

**For example:**

*Mum was **loving**, **caring**, and **compassionate**. As much as she was a **loyal**, **fun-loving** and **wise**.*

We are using some traits you have listed on Worksheet 2 – Personality Themes and Character Traits we identified earlier in your research. We are gathering those descriptions together in threes. Here we have two sets of threes together to create a rhythm to our words and to highlight what they were like as a person.

**Why The Rule of Three?**

It's known we process and understand information better in patterns. We can create a pattern using the smallest number, three. So grouping words in threes makes them more memorable. Writers, storytellers and advertisers use groups of threes. (Can you hear this in that previous sentence?) So we want to use The Rule of Three in our introduction to create a few words that are memorable about your loved one.

I've used the **Rule of Three** throughout the workbook as a stylistic device.

You may not have noticed it when you were reading, but the **Rule of Three** helps establish a rhythm to my words that can be 'heard' in your mind as you read. It will be the same when you are speaking at the funeral or memorial service. By grouping phrases, words and ideas into threes, they are pleasing on the ears and helpful in giving resonance to your words.

There is a rhythm, and a cadence of words collected together in threes. Once you know this, you will see threes everywhere, especially in speeches. It's the truth, the whole truth, and nothing but the truth, for example.

Look at your list on **Worksheet 2 – Personality Themes and Character Traits** that you identified in the research section.

We will not be using the three Key Themes we used those in the major points we have already written (we'll come back to those in a moment, in the introduction) but let's pick some others from your list.

**Applying The Rule of Three**

Here is the formula - (Mom, Dad, my Grandmother, and so on) was (1), (2) and (3). As much as he/she was (4), (5) and (6).

For example,

*Mum was loving, caring, and compassionate. As much as she was a loyal, fun-loving and wise.*

Now briefly expand on those points. Have a look at the three examples below to see how to do that.

**Step 2. Point forward to the three Key Themes you will talk about later.**

Next, in the introduction, we want to point forward to the three key themes we will talk about in our middle sections. We do this to let people know what we will say (it's the 'tell them what you're going to tell them' idea). It signals what's coming and helps as a hook for memories.

For example:

*It is impossible for me today to say everything I would want to say about Dad. He lived such a long life full of adventure, hard work, and happiness. We would need to be here for hours and still we wouldn't have scratched the surface. But in these few words, I want to remember and bring to mind how dad was adventurous (key theme A), determined (key theme B) and caring (key theme C).*

**Step 3. Introduce yourself.**

Now is the time to introduce yourself. You might think you should do this first? Most people do. But I believe saying something about the person is a much better way to start your few words instead of talking about yourself.

*For those of you who don't know me, my name is John. I'm very proud to say that Paul was my dad. It's hard to say these words today, as much as it's hard to accept he is not here.*

**Step 4. Thank You**

Last, in this introduction, we have time to say thank you.

In the basic information research section, you will have listed those people who you want to thank. Maybe for the cards, and flowers, or for someone who helped care for the person. Here is where you would also say thank you to those people who might watch a livestream of the service.

*Thank you very much for being here today to celebrate dad's life. We are so grateful for all the cards, flowers, notes and special phone calls, but above all he would have been so thankful to you all being are here to say farewell. I know that his family in Australia would so have wanted to be here today. I hope even though you are watching the service through the internet, you still can fee part of the day.*

Let's look at three examples of introductions to help you write your words. These are for a dad, a mom and a good friend. Each of these is around 150 - 200 words, which is about the length you should aim for.

*** 

**Example 1: My Dad Jim**

*Jim was traditional, conscientious and hard-working. Endearingly, we might say he was a man of his era, a bit 'old school'. He even wore a tie to do the gardening.*

*Whoever he would meet, dad would treat all with equality, patience and fairness. Yes, he was private. He didn't wear his heart on his sleeve, but once he got to know you, he was sociable and fun. Watch out! Because soon you would be on the receiving end of his wit and banter.*

*Many of you will remember his firm handshake, his sparkling eyes and rarely would you see him without his optimistic smile. I'm going to say much more about three key things that defined Jimmy – those were his kindness, generosity and humour, later.*

*My name is Steve. To most of you, he was Jim or Jimmy, but I am so proud today to call him my dad. Thank you very much for coming today to say farewell to dad... etc.*

*** 

### Example 2: My Mom Mary

*Most often, the first words you would hear when meeting Mary would be, 'Now, what can I do for you?' 'How can I help you?' 'What do you need?' That was Mary. She was as faithful, fun-loving, and wise as she was understanding, supporting, and loving.*

*She might have been small in stature, but Mary was an imposing woman with a big heart for the lost and lonely. Those perhaps others might pass by, unaware of those who are lost or overlooked in life that needed help. But not Mary. Her heart was as open as her front door. Everyone was welcome, and it was impossible to leave without eating something.*

*Simply, Mary was a remarkable woman of empathy, compassion and care, something I want to say more about today. I'm Julie, and I'm proud to say that Mary Smith was my mom. Thank you very much for coming today to say farewell to mom... etc.*

***

### Example 3: My Faithful Friend Johnno

*'Johnno' could be stubborn, hotheaded and a closed book. Fearless, loyal and dedicated, I'd met no one like him before or since. Once he decided, there was no changing his mind – ever!*

*In Latin it says, 'Utrinque Paratus.'' In English it means, 'Ready for Anything.' It's the motto of The Paras. That was him. 'Johnno' was proud to serve his country as a paratrooper for almost twenty years. I trusted 'Johnno' with my life. He always had my back.*

*'Johnno' was a man who didn't wear his heart on his sleeve. But heading into uncertainty with him by your side, you knew there was someone who would never give up on you, never abandon you, and*

*never stop fighting for you. Three things I will mention today that will be his legacy tomorrow and forever. My name is Phil, and I am so proud today to say he was my 'comrade-in-arms' for most of those twenty years. Today it is my privilege and honour to stand by his side one last time to say farewell to my best friend.*

*Thank you very much for the opportunity to say a few words about my friend John... etc.*

\*\*\*

In this simple four-part introduction process, you have done away with a throwaway opening line. Instead, you have engaging and relevant words to capture attention and point the way forward to the three key things you want to say in your words. You have identified who you are, why you are speaking, and expressed your gratitude to everyone who is there.

Once you have completed these four sections on the following worksheet, you will know what you are going to say from the first words, and it will give you confidence as you stand to speak. Now it's your turn to write the introduction.

# Chapter 21

# Worksheet 9 - Writing The Introduction

## Worksheet 9 - Writing The Introduction

Aim for about 150 - 200 words or about a third of an A4 page. The introduction should be around 10% of your total words.

**Open with the Rule of Three.**

**Point forward to the three Key Themes you will talk about later.**

**Introduce yourself.**

**Say thank you.**

# Takeaways and Actions from Step Two: DRAFT

## Important Takeaways:

- Remember this is a first draft - don't worry about getting everything perfect the first time.

- It's normal to feel overwhelmed and to believe there's more to say than can fit into the eulogy, but the first draft is there to help you focus your thoughts and ideas.

- The drafting process separates writing (getting stories and memories down, which is research) from editing (shaping these into your words). We will begin editing in the next step.

- Use the simple structure - Introduction, three Middle Sections (each focusing on a key theme about the person), and a Conclusion.

- The Introduction captures the essence of the person and may include an overriding life theme, while the Conclusion reminds everyone of the key themes and offers a final farewell.

- Each Middle Section expands on a particular theme, painting a picture of the person through stories, specific memories, and shared feelings.

- Use Rudyard Kipling's 'Six serving men' - What, Why, When, How, Where, and Who, can help to create specific and vivid memories.

## Action Points:

1. In Step Two, you will complete Worksheets 5, 6 and 7 for the three Middle sections of your words, as well as Worksheet 8 - Writing The Conclusion and Worksheet 9 - Writing The Introduction.

2. Write a draft of the three Middle Sections first, then your Conclusion, and finally your Introduction.

3. Take each section one step at a time; don't try to write everything in one go.

4. Add specific details and write what comes to mind, even if it appears random at first. It's the editing phase that will refine your words.

# STEP THREE: EDIT

# Chapter 22

# How Does Editing Craft Your First Draft into a Heartfelt Eulogy?

**You have come so far already. Well done.**

You are well on your way to bringing together a heartfelt eulogy that will be personal, authentic, and memorable.

The effort, time and energy you've given will be rewarded on the day, and afterwards as you reflect on what you have been able to do in paying tribute to your loved one or friend.

In this section, we will bring together all the work you have done so far, and create a full version of your words ready for rehearsal.

**In step one**, you collected lots of research information. Some you have used, some you can keep for the future.

**In step two**, you narrowed those memories and stories into a simple eulogy structure.

**In step three**, we now bring a final version of what you have done so far together.

The purpose of the first draft is to get the words out of your head. Your first draft is only that – a draft. All first drafts need a little editing.

When we edit, we find odd words we don't need, or phrases we repeat, that we can remove. We rewrite the words, and when we do, we may add a few more, or break them down into difference sentences and paragraphs.

**Remember, your aim is – 'I want to say a few words.'**

We are writing to speak, not for someone to read. How it sounds matters. Not if every sentence is perfect English with exact grammar. We don't speak like that. Your words should sound like you speak, and not like someone else's English essay.

What do you edit? These are ways you can sharpen and refine your words when editing.

**Spotting Words and Phrases To Remove or Change**

Here's some words, phrases and patterns you might want to spot and edit by changing, or removing them.

**Adverbs** — Do you have many adverbs? Adverbs are words ending in '– LY.' They can be helpful, but don't overuse them. Think of another way to say the word.

**Long Sentences** — Do you have long sentences? Shorter, snappy sentences can be easier to say, (which helps with you when speaking), and have a better rhythm on the ears. Find ways of varying the length so you can add pauses for a breath and to make a point more noticeable.

**Tautologies** — Can you cut out any words? Tautologies are words and phrases that mean the same thing. So, for example, 'biography of his life' could be biography. You don't need both.

Another common phrase to edit is 'have got.' You can use either, have or got, rather than both words.

Do you repeat the same words? Try not to use 'really,' 'very' and 'just.'

What about the phrases 'sort of, or kind of?'

Rather than using 'it' can you use a more specific word?

Do you have many 'filler words?' For example, 'each and everyone,' 'When it comes to,' or 'At the end of the day.' You may be able to edit some or all of these.

**Listen To Your Words**

Here's a great tip to help with editing - get the computer to speak your words to you.

On most word processing programmes, there is an option to hear the words being read by the computer. This is an excellent way of editing. Try the Edit menu, see if you can find it there.

By listening to the words two or three times you can hear the rhythm of the sentences, spot those too long, and certain phrases will not resonate with you when you hear them, and it's so easy to miss that when you are only writing the words. Try it.

If time will allow, let the words you have written sit for a while. Even if it is only overnight. When we come back to words we have written, we see them differently. It always helps to have a break between your drafting and editing.

By now, you will have these worksheets completed with your stories, memories, and thoughts in a draft.

- Introduction

- Section 1 – (From key theme A)

- Section 2 – (From key theme B)
- Section 3 – (From key theme C)
- Conclusion

Let's start with the worksheet for the introduction.

If you have written your words on a computer, it may be helpful to print your words out. Somehow, working on paper is more helpful at this stage.

Now read out loud your introduction slowly from your first word to your last. Saying your words out loud helps the most in editing.

How does it sound as you read? Are there phrases or sentences you stumble on as you say them, like a tricky tongue twister? Make a note of them. Circle them or underline them.

Why not use the voice memo app on most smartphones these days and record yourself as you read the words aloud? Don't be anxious or self-conscious about this. It is only you who will hear them at this stage. You can do this in private without feeling embarrassed. It is all good practice for when you will say them at the service.

**Editing Checklist**

- Do your words sound like how you would speak?
- Can you cut some words to say the same in less?
- Are there clichés which sound unnatural when you hear them?
- Do any phrases sound confusing?
- Does it sound as if it flows?
- Have your words got a natural rhythm?

Now rewrite your edited introduction.

Don't forget to check your final word count. Remember, aim to speak for 7-8 mins at 115 - 130 words a minute, which is around 1000 - 12000 words or about one and a half to two A4 pages in size 12 font, single spaced.

After making any changes you need to make, rewrite the final version on worksheet 10 – Bringing Your Words Together. This will be your final version.

Now repeat the process above for sections 1, 2, 3, and your conclusion. When you have done this, delete the headings for the sections, only leaving the words you have written.

It always feels like we could edit more and more. However, if you have worked through the sections this far, by now you will have a short eulogy speech that will be specific, structured and memorable.

Well done. It will reward the work you have done with a sense that you have done the best you can do for the person. Your few words will be a lasting gift to them and everyone who is there to hear them at the service. Now we need to move on to a critical part of the process: step four – rehearsal.

# Chapter 23

## WORKSHEET 10 – BRINGING YOUR WORDS TOGETHER

### Introduction

(COPY YOUR EDITED WORDS from your Introduction section here.)

**Transition:**

# Section 1

(Copy your edited words from key theme A here.)

**Transition:**

# Section 2

(Copy your edited words from key theme B here.)

**Transition:**

# Section 3

(Copy your edited words from key theme C here.)

**Transition:**

# Conclusion

(Copy your edited words from your conclusion section here.)

# Takeaways and Actions from Step Three: EDIT

## Important Takeaways:

- Editing is an important step in creating your heartfelt words of eulogy. This is when you shape your final version.

- The first draft is only a draft, is editing that helps to refine the words and make them sound like how you speak.

- Editing involves removing unnecessary words and phrases, varying sentence length, and avoiding repetition.

- Reading your words out loud or using the computer's read-aloud feature can help with editing.

- After editing, rewrite the final version on the worksheet and aim for a word count of around 1000 words.

## Action Points:

1. Edit your Introduction, Section 1, Section 2, Section 3 and Conclusion separately.

2. Rewrite the full final version on Worksheet 10 - Bringing Your Words Together.

3. Use the computer's read-aloud feature and record yourself reading your words out loud.

4. Check your final word count to aim for 7-8 minutes of speaking time.

# STEP FOUR: REHEARSAL

# Chapter 24

# WHY IS REHEARSING YOUR EULOGY A KEY STEP IN THE PROCESS?

ARE YOU NERVOUS ABOUT saying your few words? Don't be surprised if you are. That's only natural. But coming this far in the process will help you prepare the words to say. Now we are at the stage of rehearsing them.

You are the same as nearly everyone else. Most people in the world have speaking in public as one of their biggest fears. Standing in front of any group of people and speaking to them will cause adrenaline to surge through your body – the 'fight or flight" reaction impossible to avoid.

But taking a few simple steps to rehearse your words beforehand can minimise as much as possible those feelings of anxiety, helping you speak with confidence, clarity, and conviction. The time you spend here in rehearsing your words will pay dividends on the day of the funeral or memorial service.

**Four Rehearsal Steps To Ease Nerves On The Day**

**1 – Print Out A Final Rehearsal Version**

By now, you will have a final edited version of your words. Depending on how you have written these words, it may be on a computer or by hand. Now I would recommend you create a version on a word processor ready to print.

- Create a rehearsal copy at least size 14 font and 1.5 spaced lines.

- Use a clearly legible Sans serif font, such as Verdana. Sans serif fonts stand out on a page better to read from a distance. Enlarging the font will help you see the words from a distance. You don't want to be holding the paper when you speak.

- Write at the top of each page – **SLOW DOWN**. Nervousness on the day will make you speed up when you speak. Reminding yourself to take a breath if needed and slow your speech so everyone can hear what you are saying is so helpful in the moment.

- Number your pages. This is an important step. If you should drop your papers, or they come apart (and it happens), there is no panic to find your place again quickly and easily.

- Print it single sided. Having text only on one side of the paper makes moving from page to page simpler. Also, sometimes, the reversed text shading through from the other side can be a distraction.

## 2 – Read It Out Loud At Least Three Times

Go somewhere private or where you won't feel conscious about reading your words out loud.

First time, read the complete document out loud. As we did earlier, record yourself if you can.

How did it flow as you spoke the words out loud?

Listen back to the recording if you did one. Did anything stick out as sounding stumbled over or too wordy?

Now, should you need to make any changes, edit the text. Remembering to save this new version.

Now read the amended version out loud **a second time**.

Sometimes we trip over words when we say them out loud. Better to find another way of saying the same thing with a different choice of word. Every time you edit words, it is an investment in how you will sound on the day. Trust me - it's not time wasted.

Make a note of your start and stop times. How long did it take to read? Are you close to your target time? Are you speaking within a range of 115 -130 words per minute? If you notice a significant difference, could it be because you're reading too fast or too slow?

How does that sound now after a second read through? If you need any odd tweaks, make them.

Create a further third version of the document with any more changes you have made, and print another copy.

Now rehearse again for a third time with a final read through out loud and **standing up**.

You will stand when you speak on the day. Putting yourself in the same position rehearsing will help. It's almost like your tongue gets muscle memory, getting used to saying the words. You should not need to make any more changes after reading the eulogy a third time, but don't worry if you do. Now is the time to edit.

## 3 – Overlearn Your Opening and Closing Sentences

Thinking back over the work you have completed, you will remember the importance of the opening and closing words of a speech. I find the technique of overlearning these first and last couple of sentences of immense value.

**What do I mean by overlearning?**

It is not committing these lines to memory, but similar. By reading them repeatedly and speaking them out loud, you will feel more natural saying them on the day, and the words will flow easier. It helps you settle down into speaking as you know these first couple of sentences so well.

In addition, it allows you to end your words with confidence and conviction. Often when speaking, people fade towards the end of their words, relieved that the end is coming. But for the many reasons we looked at, now is the time to speak with certainty and confidence in your voice. Overlearning your closing lines will do that for you.

**4 – Print A Final Version And Practice, Practice, Practice**

That's it.

If you've made any final adjustments, create a final version with no written comments or alterations, and you have finished. Depending on how much time you have before the funeral or memorial service, try to read it once a day beforehand. Out loud and standing up. Every time you do, it will reward you with fewer nerves during the day.

# Chapter 25

# How to Stand Strong When Saying Your Words

## Saying Your Few Words With Confidence and Clarity on the Day

When the day arrives, if you have followed all these steps, you will have a few words to say which are considered, structured and well-rehearsed. There is nothing more you could have done to honour the memory of your loved one.

Here are a few more thoughts and actions you can take for saying your words on the day of the funeral or memorial service.

**Preparation on the Day**

- Make sure you have the printed version of your words in a place you will see them. Put your car keys on top of them, store them in your bag or put them in the folder you will take with you. A last-minute issue or panic could see you run out the door without them. I see that happen more times than you can imagine.

- Before you are about to speak, take a few deep, long breaths to calm your nervous system down. The same as you walk to take your place at the front. It's OK to walk a little slower towards the front as well; all these things will bring a sense of calm. Everything will help.

**During the Eulogy**

- Standing at the podium or lectern, pause before you speak and scan the people there. Look around the room, making eye contact, and then, taking a big breath, begin those first lines. Now you will sense the benefit of overlearning those words, as they will flow easily and you will get into your stride.

- Speak slowly and don't rush your words. Remember the **SLOW DOWN** at the top of the page.

- Pause between paragraphs. Take a breath.

- Don't worry if you get emotional saying the words. Don't apologise. You have nothing to say sorry about. Everyone there will root for you. Trust me, they will. Stop. Take a breath. Wait. When the moment passes and it will, then continue.

- Be yourself. Don't change the sound of your voice. Read the words as if you were talking to the person. Though hard, say some of your farewells by looking at the coffin.

- Remember, the person who you are speaking about would be so proud of you.

- It's such a beautiful gift you are giving them. Everyone there is rooting for you. When you speak from your heart of someone you love, people will always remember that. Someone needs to do this, and it's you that has the courage. You've put in the work. Well done.

- It's not embarrassing if you fill with emotion. Take a breath, gather yourself and carry on.

- As you reach the end, say, 'Thank you'. Again, pause a little before you walk back to your seat. No need to rush back.

You have been able to complete the thing you wished the most, to 'say a few words' about a loved one at their funeral.

## What do you say to people after the service?

I've always found the best reply to someone saying, 'You did great, well done, is to say, 'thank you, that's kind of you to say.'

Don't add how nervous you felt. Or how you wish you could have done better. We do those things to hide a little embarrassment or nervousness.

You will have spent hours in researching, writing a first draft, editing and rehearsal. While I'm not saying you should be conceited, you should be proud of what you have achieved.

You will have done what so many people wished they had or could have done.

You took courage, invested the time, and created memorable words to say in a eulogy.

And that is an outstanding achievement. Well done.

# Takeaways and Actions from REHEARSAL

## Important Takeaways:

- Public speaking, especially at a funeral or memorial service, will a be worrying time. But you can help this a little by proper preparation and rehearsal.

- Four main steps for rehearsal include printing out a legible, large-font version of the speech, reading the speech out loud multiple times, overlearning the opening and closing lines, and practicing repeatedly.

- The physical format of the speech (font size, type, single-sided printing, and numbering) can aid in the ease of delivery.

- Overlearning opening and closing lines can help start and end the speech with confidence.

- Repeated practice helps to reduce nerves and improve the flow of speech.

- On the day of the event, a combination of preparation and mindful actions can help manage nerves and deliver your heartfelt eulogy with confidence and pride for a loved one.

## Action Points:

1. Print out a final version of the speech in a large, legible font, single-sided and numbered.

2. Read the speech out loud at least three times, making adjustments for flow and timing as needed.

3. Overlearn the opening and closing lines of the speech to ensure a confident start and finish.

4. Practice the speech regularly before the event, standing up as you would on the day.

5. On the day, take deep breaths, walk slowly, and pause before starting your speech to manage nerves.

6. After the speech, accept compliments graciously and take pride in your accomplishment.

# Chapter 26

## CLOSING THOUGHTS

I WISH YOU STRENGTH and courage as the day draws near. It is a beautiful thing you are doing.

As a eulogy speechwriter and funeral celebrant with over 10 years of experience, I use these same steps weekly, speaking to families who have lost a loved one. These are methods I know work.

For me, it is always the highest of compliments when someone asks me following a funeral, 'How long did you know John?' It surprises them when I reply, 'I've never met him.' This four-step process can help me sound as if I knew him. Of course, it's not quite the same as knowing them, but the process helps me find words that are relevant and meaningful.

But for you and your family, it will be so different now you have written your words. Now, you will say those memorable words on the day as someone who knew and loved the person. That will be of great comfort to everyone at the funeral or memorial service. As much, it will be of immense comfort to you.

Why? I see healing, comfort and a sense of pride after people have spoken at the funeral or memorial service.

I'm sure you will feel the same. Scared stiff of standing and speaking now, but afterwards forever grateful you did.

Feel you need more help? Please check through the wealth of information and resources in the following **Common Questions and Bonus Resources** section.

If you would like to contact me, ask for more advice, please visit www.memorablewords.co.uk or www.peterbillingham.com. There you will find my contact details.

At the end of the workbook, you will find a section explaining the editing and rewriting services I offer if you would like further help.

Thank you very much for purchasing this eulogy writing toolkit—I Want to Say a Few Words: How To Craft a Heartfelt Eulogy for a Loved One's Funeral.

With gratitude,

**Peter Billingham**

# Common Questions & Bonus Resources

# Chapter 27

## COMMON QUESTIONS & BONUS RESOURCES CONTENTS

### Common Questions

- What is a eulogy?
- What do I feel I want to say a few words?
- What information should I include in a eulogy?
- How long should a eulogy be?
- How should I structure the eulogy?
- Why bother preparing a few words to say?
- What makes a eulogy memorable?
- Should I use a poem in a eulogy?

### Bonus Worksheets

- Bonus Worksheet 1 - The Lifeline Exercise
- Bonus Worksheet 2 - Life Lessons and Legacy
- Bonus Worksheet 3 - 10 Overriding Life Theme Eulogy Titles & Quotations
- Bonus Worksheet 4 - 36 Extra Memory Prompt Questions
- Bonus Worksheet 5 - 26 Quotations For Telling A Life Story
- Bonus Worksheet 6 - Family & Friends Questionnaire

# Common Questions

### WHAT IS A EULOGY?

A eulogy is the words spoken about a person at their funeral or celebration of life service.

The meaning of the word eulogy is a speech of 'good words'. From its Greek roots, it means a speech of 'praise'.

Writing a eulogy involves finding specific, authentic and relevant words to describe the values, personality traits and themes of a life. It's remembering stories of times shared and what the person meant to you.

A eulogy helps everyone at the funeral or memorial service bring back to mind happy memories of the person, the life they lived and the legacy they leave behind.

It is a speech of kind words, thankful thoughts, and precious memories.

### Why Do I Feel I Want To Say A Few Words?

Some people feel the need to speak about a loved one at a funeral, while others don't.

Loss, and how we experience and deal with it, is an individual process. What feels a priority for some does not need to be expressed by another. You can't judge how another person feels about this, only to know that you feel you want to speak.

One thing I have learned in writing over 700 eulogies is we all deal with loss differently. For some people, it becomes important to say a few words, however hard they feel it will be to do, while others find the opposite. For them, being quiet, reflecting and supporting others is the best way forward for them.

Saying a few words can be a wonderful way to honour someone's life. As the years pass, you will be so thankful, and at peace about the day you said farewell to someone you loved by saying a few words. It will be a blessing for others in your family, too. You will put into words what other people are feeling but can't find the words to say.

### What Information Should I Include In A Eulogy?

Keep this simple idea in mind. Imagine you are sitting alone with the person who has died.

- What would you say to them?

- What would you want to thank them for?

- In what ways would you express your love to and for them?

- How would you tell them what they mean to you?
- What is different in your life because of them?
- How have you learned about life, work, friendship, love and relationships from them?
- How will you miss them?

Keeping the words simple, not being worried about 'giving a speech' but sharing what you think and how you feel makes a eulogy focused and also makes it memorable.

**How Long Should A Eulogy Be?**

Saying a few words at a funeral is often restricted by time. Many funeral services they limit to around thirty minutes at crematoriums in England. It is impossible to say everything you want to say, no matter how much time you will have.

I recommend for most people who will want to give a eulogy, around 6-8 minutes is about the right time. This gives enough time to have an introduction, middle sections to share memories and stories, and a conclusion to finish.

We speak around 130-150 words a minute. Often, because of understandable nervousness, we speak faster – too fast sometimes. When delivering your few words, intentionally slow the pace of your voice.

As a guideline, eight minutes speaking at a pace of 115 words a minute is about 920 words or around two A4 pages of text. To work out how many words to write, use this calculation. Words divided by the time you want to speak. An A4 page with size 12 font is about 400 words.

**How Should I Structure The Eulogy?**

Having a simple structure to write your words is like having a map for a journey. You know where you are starting from and where you will end. It will guide your thoughts and the direction of your research, and you will know when you have enough words to say.

The most effective structure for any speech is in three parts. 'Tell them what you're going to tell them, tell them and tell them what you've told them' is an adage used for centuries.

This toolkit will help you say those few words that have an introduction, three main points in the body of your words and then a conclusion.

**How Long Does It Take To Write A Eulogy?**

My advice is don't rush writing a eulogy. However, with the date of the funeral or memorial service days away, time may feel and be short.

Writing a eulogy involves three key stages — research, drafting and editing.

From experience, the more time you spend in research, the stages of drafting and editing needs less. Collecting the memories takes the most time.

You need to give yourself the gift of time.

Writing these words is not like writing an essay or business proposal. Thinking about a loved one you have lost will be emotional and bring many feelings to the surface. For many people, it is cathartic. There comes a sense of healing and help in writing the words.

**As a guideline, it will take about an hour of preparation for every minute you speak.** You might think that sounds excessive, but from writing hundreds of eulogies, I know it takes time.

Trying to speak at a funeral unprepared, I've seen people freeze on the spot and not know what to say, or speak about irrelevant things, or keep speaking until I've had to tell them to stop.

Remember, you will never get a second chance. Every hour you spend in preparation is worth it on the day.

**Why Bother Preparing A Few Words To Say?**

Some people say, 'I don't need to plan and prepare, I'll think of what I'm going to say on the day', hoping inspiration comes to them at the moment. Don't do this.

Walking to the front of the chapel or funeral home, you stand at the lectern and there, a few feet away, is a coffin. In front of you are family and friends.

Your body will flood with adrenaline and it can cloud your mind and make your tongue feel as if it is about five inches thick. Don't take the risk of either of those scenarios taking place.

Set aside the time, take the steps in the toolkit and you will end up with a memorable eulogy at the funeral service or celebration of life of a loved one.

**What Makes A Eulogy Memorable?**

Being memorable is not the eloquence of the speaker or writing impressive words. But the three key aspects to remember when saying a few words are to be **authentic**, **sincere**, and **specific**. Keep the few words you want to say as simple as possible.

Don't make the person sound as if they were bordering on being a saint if they were not. Perhaps refrain from using religious language if the person was not someone with a faith. Being sincere is saying what comes from the heart with any absence of pretence.

Does that mean your words need to be warts and all? No, definitely not. This is not the time or place to air grievances or criticise or condemn.

Last, making the words memorable is finding specifics. Be specific in the stories, memories, and relevant descriptions. It is the smallest specific details that will allow your words not to be filled with cliches or generalisations.

For example, you could say, 'Mum loved perfume.' Or you could reminisce, 'As mum hugged you, there was always the fragrance of Youth-Dew by Estée Lauder mixed in with the warmth you felt inside.'

Repeating the exact catchphrases and the descriptions of their mannerisms all helps to make the few words you say memorable, not only for you but for everyone there.

Try to understand the viewpoints of the people there. Are there only family or are there friends and work colleagues? You may need to give some thoughts to memories from those as well.

**Should I Use a Poem in A Eulogy?**

Yes, maybe a few stanzas from a poem can say so much of how you are feeling. Putting into words your emotions and summing up how you think and remember, they can capture a loved one or friend in using a poem to start or end a eulogy.

Poetry is such a personal and individual choice. What may sound sentimental and meaningful to one person feels twee and overemotional to another.

A simple search on the internet for funeral poems will bring up many sites full of poetry to choose from.

Always give reference to the author when using a poem. Here are several worth finding online and considering.

- Death is Nothing at All by Henry Scott Holland
- Do Not Go Gentle into That Good Night by Dylan Thomas
- She/He is Gone by David Harkins
- Remember Me When I Am Gone Away by Christina Rossetti
- On Death by Kahlil Gibran
- Epitaph on my Own Friend by Robert Burns
- Farewell my Friends by Rabindranath Tagore
- Afterglow by Helen Lowrie Marshall

# Chapter 28

# BONUS WORKSHEET 1 – THE LIFELINE EXERCISE

## How Can the Lifeline Exercise Enhance Your Heartfelt Eulogy?

PLOTTING OUT A SIMPLE 'lifeline' representing key moments, the 'ups and downs' of life, can sometimes be a helpful tool in thinking through what could be important to add to the eulogy. It can help you gather insights about the person and the shape of the story of their life.

There is a debate about nature versus nurture. Are we a product of our genes or our experiences? Do our genes and hereditary factors influence our lives? Or, are they the childhood experiences, the cultural environment we live in, and our relationships that shape us to become the people others will remember?

The people we are, our identity, are, of course, shaped by many factors. Plotting out the shape of a life can sometimes reveal seasons, trends, and reasons for developing particular individual traits and characteristics.

**How to Plot the Lifeline**

On a plain A4 page in landscape, mark the beginning with their date of birth on the left-hand side and the end point as the date of their passing on the right-hand side.

Now split the lifeline into sections representing every five-year interval. Add into the lifeline key moments and turning points, plotting a point as a 'High' or 'Low' point.

**Looking For Key Life Moments**

For example:

- Childhood years: Were there any significant events that shaped their early years?
- Finding a best friend: When and how did they meet their lifelong companions?
- Leaving school: Was this a turning point in their life?
- Further education or landing their first job: How did this phase shape their professional career?

- Meeting their life partner: When and how did they meet their significant other?

- Birth of children: How did becoming a parent change them?

- Job promotions or career changes: How did their career progress and what impact did it have on them?

- Meeting a mentor or significant friend: Who were the people that greatly influenced them?

- Fantastic adventures or significant achievements: What were their high points and victories?

- Losing a loved one or facing redundancy: How did they cope with major losses or setbacks?

- Health issues or serious accidents: How did they handle health crises or accidents?

- Relationship changes: How did changes in personal relationships affect them?

- Retirement: How did they transition into this phase?

- Arrival of grandchildren: How did becoming a grandparent alter their perspective?

- Major life lessons or changes: What were the pivotal moments that significantly changed their life course?

**As you plot these key moments, also consider:**

- Was their life mainly filled with 'High or Low' points?

- Did they keep moving forward or stop when obstacles came their way?

- How did the challenges of life shape them?

- Would you describe their life as an upward trend – not starting well, but ending beautifully?

- Was it a 'rags to riches' life or vice versa?

- Did they overcome an illness that changed their life's course?

- Was a job lost, was a fortune misplaced, or was an opportunity missed?

- Do any patterns or themes emerge from their life events?

**Reflecting on Life's Highs and Lows**

Remember, the aim of this exercise is not to judge or evaluate, but to understand and appreciate the unique journey of their life.

Everyone's life story is unique, filled with moments of joy, happiness, trials, and sadness. Rather than looking for what you might consider the 'right' answer, stay curious and open to what you might discover.

Circumstances happening beyond our control can force us to change. How we respond or react to life's highs and lows writes chapters in the story of our life.

Out of tragic situations can come opportunity. From painful seasons, we can gain gratitude for the joyful ones.

Often it is these moments which are the moments of defining change. Testing our character, making us the people we become and who people remember.

# Chapter 29

# Bonus Worksheet 2 – Life Lessons and Legacy

> I hold that a strongly marked personality can influence descendants for generations.
> Beatrix Potter

How are you different today because of the person you want to say a few words about? We can often learn more from observing how a life was lived than by being instructed how to live a life.

How will you remember your loved one who you want to write a few words about? How have they influenced your life?

If they were your parent, at a DNA hereditary level, in every cell they still live – but now in you. They will live on too, into generations of their descendants. So, what will be their legacy?

Here are some questions to prompt memories and thoughts about their legacy.

## Character Traits

- Can you see their influence in you? In what ways? How do their values, attitudes, or speech show up in your life?
- Do you have some of the same personality themes and character traits? Which ones?
- Are you similar in ways that bring you comfort and peace, knowing you are like them? Try to put into words how you feel.

## Values and Principles

- How do you respond to situations similar to them? Can you see their compassion, kindness, and care in your altruistic actions? What specific instances come to mind?
- Do you support the same charities, or volunteer in similar organisations?

- Do you carry forward their principles of justice, respect, and integrity? How, and in what way?

**Shared Experience**

- Is there a particular life event or experience where their influence or support was pivotal?

- What is the greatest lesson you have learned from them?

**Legacy**

- How will you remember them? Remember, legacy is much more about leaving something in people, rather than leaving something for people.

- How would you define their legacy? If you could say anything to them, what would it be?

- How would you express your gratitude for their influence, support, or love that they infused into your life?

As you reflect on these questions, remember not every question will apply to everyone, and that's OK. These are merely prompts designed to spark reflection and recall memories. Can answering any of these questions help your eulogy?

# Chapter 30

## BONUS WORKSHEET 3 – 10 OVERRIDING LIFE THEMES

### Can having an overriding life theme help you when writing a eulogy?

HAVING AN OVERRIDING LIFE theme for a eulogy can help provide structure and focus, making the words you say memorable. It's not required, but in the right circumstances, it can help you build your words around a life theme using a title and having a quote to match.

It is common these days to have a printed order of service at a funeral or a memorial service. By building the few words you say around an overriding life theme, and adding a quotation as a memory hook, in the future people will more likely remember what you said about the person. It will come to mind all over again when rereading the order of service booklet. The title and the theme will bring back your words about the person to their memory.

You can research an overriding life theme at every step of the process. However, when you complete Worksheet 2 - Personality Themes and Character Traits — you may notice one repeating idea or theme comes to mind more often than others. This could be the one to choose.

By searching on the internet for quotes, poems or saying about that personality theme, you will find something perfect for your words.

### Creating Your Own Themes and Quotations

Following are ten titles and quotations I've used in writing eulogies. I've also added a few notes to help you with the type of personalities, characteristics and themes and situations they represented.

Some descriptions and situations may resonate with the words you want to write. Please freely use them if you can. Or take ideas from mine to create your own themes and find quotations to enhance them. You can find inspiration by drawing from the list of themes, personalities and characteristics you discovered in the research step about the person the eulogy is about.

Now explore the following list of eulogy titles, quotations, and associated personality traits and themes to see if any might work for your words.

# Title: You Could Never Take That Unceasing Shine Away

Quotation by Walt Whitman

'Some people are so much sunshine to the square inch.'

**Eulogy themes.**

- Resilience.

- Determination.

- Smile.

- Overcoming.

- Determined.

- Resolute.

**Character Descriptions**

You can describe resilience as having the ability to adapt to difficult situations. When illness, stress, adversity or trauma strikes, and you experience anger, grief and pain, but you keep going, regardless.

This overriding theme would be suitable for a person where a debilitating illness, MS, or a terminal illness, for example, was ravaging their finite days, devastating their body, but cruelly leaving their mind intact. Yet it seemed nothing could ever take away the light in their heart and soul. That's how you could describe their resilience.

This theme could be for someone who smiled despite what unjust things happened. Showing how they overcame unfair obstacles in life yet remaining optimistic. The glass of their life was always full and overflowing. Facing challenges with soul level strength and never without a smile.

Tragedy happened. Misfortune arrived. Yet despite this, they could find a place to still smile at life. They overcame significant personal health problems or perhaps showed resilience while caring for a loved one. A stoic person who suffered but kept a smile, regardless.

\*\*\*

# Title: A Friend Who Held Life Together

Quotation by Jon Katz:

'I think if I've learned anything about friendship, it's to hang in, stay connected, fight for them, and let them fight for you. Don't walk away, don't be distracted, don't be too busy or tired, don't take them for granted. Friends are part of the glue that holds life and faith together.'

**Eulogy themes**.

- Friendship.
- Companionship.
- Loyalty.
- Support.
- Kindness.
- Trustworthy.
- Confidant.

## Character Descriptions

Were they the type of person to put friendship above all else?

Then, this overriding theme would be especially suitable for them. Friendship was of the utmost importance to them, it was a core value they upheld.

You would describe them as loyal and dependable, and always ready to come to your aid no matter what the circumstance.

If you ever need someone to talk to, someone to give you advice, or a shoulder to cry on and a good laugh, they were the first person you know was always there for you. They were as dependable as a rock.

They may not have always agreed with you, but you knew and never doubted they had your back. These days, we may add the initialism, they were your Bff. A friend in whom you could confide, with whom you could trust your thoughts. You could share your deepest, darkest secrets with them and they would never tell a soul.

They were the friend who was there through it all - your highs and lows. They were the one with whom you shared so much of your life.

***

# Title: Greater Than Riches

Quotation by Henry Fielding

'I am content; that is a blessing greater than riches; and he to whom that is given need ask no more.'

**Eulogy themes.**

- Contentment.
- Gratitude.
- Joy.
- Happiness.
- Satisfied.
- Ease.

**Character Descriptions**

If you have more, so marketers tell us, more money, more beauty, more stuff, then happiness will ensue. But does having things equal happiness? For some, the resounding answer is no.

This theme is for those who don't go along with materialism and consumerism, and locate that hard-to-find butterfly of bliss and contentment with not much. Not much by the world's standards, perhaps, but they were rich in contentment.

They have found genuine joy and contentment in life, no matter their circumstances or their situation. Just as they are. Whatever they possess, it is more than enough. Never envious of others' possessions or situations, they were grateful for what life had given them, living happily and fulfilled each day.

Life was full of blessings, and there was no desire to alter it in any way. Being themselves and being in that specific place and time was enough to satisfy them. These same people often display qualities such as compassion, dedication to their families, and a willingness to put the needs of others before their own.

***

# Title: It's What We Do That Matters

Quotation by Germany Kent

'Live your life in such a way that you'll be remembered for your kindness, compassion, fairness, character, benevolence, and a force for good who had much respect for life, in general.'

**Eulogy themes.**

- Unselfish.
- Altruistic.
- Caring.
- Action.
- Devotion.
- Serving.

**Character Descriptions**

Many people talk about doing good things, but stand on the sidelines looking in. Feeling sad, but spectating on the sorrows of others. This theme is for someone opposite in attitude. They could not help themselves, wanting to help others.

This person was someone who acted each day to bring positive change to the world. Either by giving of time to serve as a volunteer, or sharing the resources of time or skills. Many others might not even have known about their acts of altruism, as they often performed these in secret.

This person was proactive. They saw a need in someone's life and gave practical or emotional help. Perhaps serving in the community as a volunteer or as a friendly neighbour. This altruistic attitude was the hallmark of their life.

Living unselfishly, showing compassion to all in both giving of time and resources to help others, they were people who everyone knew as kind, caring and supporting willing to help others.

Living for others in this manner brought them a life of fulfilment and happiness.

***

# Title: Beautiful People Don't Just Happen

Quotation by Elisabeth Kübler-Ross

'The most beautiful people we have known are those who have known defeat, known suffering, known struggle, known loss, and have found their way out of the depths. These persons have an appreciation, a sensitivity, and an understanding of life that fills them with compassion, gentleness, and a deep loving concern. Beautiful people do not just happen.'

**Eulogy themes.**

- Resilience.
- Overcoming.
- Compassion.
- Loss.
- Tragedy.
- Stoicism.

**Character Descriptions**

Why is it we often ask 'why' when we witness injustice, intolerance, or random tragedies in the lives of people around us? Bad things happen to good people. Life can be unexplainable and cruel.

Viktor Frankl is one of my favourite authors. No matter how many times I read Man's Search for Meaning, Frankl's famous book, it fills me with inspiration and hope. It has many themes you can use, for example. Frankl writes, 'Everything can be taken from a man but one thing: the last of the human freedoms—to choose one's attitude in any given set of circumstances, to choose one's own way.'

This person's life theme was that they were someone who held on tight to the last of the human freedoms - the freedom to choose one's own way. They chose their own attitude. Choosing to become beautiful rather than bitter.

Perhaps this person endured great sadness in their life, such as the loss of a loved one. Perhaps they lived with a debilitating illness. Maybe even they had a disability. Maybe a tragic event would change the circumstances of their life forever in a moment?

Yet somehow, rather than reacting and becoming bitter or miserable, they responded by using the difficult situation to make themselves better, kinder, and compassionate. Facing overwhelming loss, sadness or pain made them someone of beauty and compassion instead.

***

# Title: Love Endures

Quotation by Kaleb Kilton

'They say love is eternal... They say love is enduring. It always protects, always trusts, always hopes, always perseveres. Love never fails... There is a quality about that kind of love that transcends our mortal understanding.'

**Eulogy themes.**

- Love.
- Relationship.
- Commitment.
- Faithfulness.
- Life partner.
- Soulmate.

**Character Descriptions**

Some relationships are instantaneous and unceasing. A marriage or partnership that's lasted through thick and thin. This theme is for such a relationship.

The two people clicked. The world was the same for them. They even would sing the same songs.

Some couples are like the pieces of a jigsaw that fit in place. This overriding theme is for when one of those partners in a connected couple passes away.

Happiness and joy being together filled them and spilt over the side of their hearts. While it was all love, it wasn't always easy. It wasn't all simple. Some rain must fall into every life. Despite being surrounded by love, those who are rich in it can still feel the hardships of life.

No matter what the cruel hands of fate may have dealt certain cards into their lives, nothing would ever come between the incredible love and bond that they shared.

This couple shared between them the greatest thing of all. They embraced the warmth of the love they shared and the knowledge that being devoted to each other was all that mattered.

While they now may be apart, death will never separate them. Love never dies.

This theme would be suitable for a couple who loved each other for many years. So many years that instead of being two separate people, they became one person with two parts.

***

# Title: Always There

Quotation by Marty Rubin

'Be there when the dawn breaks, when the first waves come in. Be there.'

**Eulogy themes.**

- Parenthood.

- Grandparents.

- Dependability.

- Selflessness.

- Paternal.

- Caring.

**Character Descriptions**

Often one of the first things people say when speaking about a parent, or grandparent, is they were always there. What does it mean to have that feeling of safety and knowing we were not alone? I think it nurtures self-confidence and self-assurance. It develops a powerful sense of personal awareness.

Sadly, not everyone grows up with parents whose presence is always physically there. For many reasons, children might have had to come home from school to an empty house. It could be the challenge to get the difficult balance of support and care throughout childhood and adolescence, while still working to support a home. A single parent, maybe.

Presence is much more than being there in person. A parent or grandparent could have made childhood a place of safety, security and, above all, fun, and still worked full-time. That itself is a major achievement.

While physical presence is undeniably important, it's also essential to recognise that emotional availability and support can be as impactful, if not more. A parent's or grandparent's consistent emotional presence can turn a house into a home, even if work or other obligations prevent them from being there physically at all times.

This theme is more about a feeling of always having someone there at the end of a phone call or to visit and offer a wise word of advice or a shoulder to cry on. Knowing, no matter what, they would always love you. The focus of this overriding life theme echoes of someone who always thought about you first and themselves second.

***

# Title: Comprehending The Mystery Every Day

Quotation by Albert Einstein

'The important thing is not to stop questioning. Curiosity has its own reason for existing. One cannot help but be in awe when one contemplates the mysteries of eternity, of life, of the marvellous structure of reality. It is enough if one tries to comprehend only a little of this mystery every day.'

**Eulogy themes.**

- Curiosity.
- Knowledge.
- Fascination.
- Awe.
- Education.
- Dedication.

**Character Descriptions**

Some people never lose the awe of life. They're inquisitive folks who maintain a sense of awe and respect for life, whatever it brings. No matter how many years pass. It seems within them there is an unquenchable desire to learn and grow in knowledge and skills. For them, age is merely a number. Never a barrier to expand their horizons.

The French Psychologist Marie de Hennezel wrote a captivating book called, 'The Warmth of The Heart Prevents The Body from Rusting.' It's about a few distinctive individuals who savour the golden years of life, seeming to never advance in age, always remaining curious about life. This theme is for one of those who aged but didn't become old, keeping that heart and spirit they had throughout life. Each day for them is a new day to develop and grow their knowledge and skills.

It is for someone who finds solace and joy in studying a subject. Perhaps dedicating themselves to a cause or artistic passion. A person who never stopped learning, never stopped growing, and celebrating with the joy of knowledge.

\*\*\*

# Title: The Quiet Hero

Quotation by George R. R. Martin

'My own heroes are the dreamers, those men and women who tried to make the world a better place than when they found it, whether in small ways or great ones. Some succeeded, some failed, most had mixed results... but it is the effort that's heroic, as I see it.'

**Eulogy themes.**

- Unassuming.
- Courage.
- Resilience.
- Overcoming.
- Resolute.
- Gutsy.

**Character Descriptions**

Faster than a speeding bullet. More powerful than a locomotive. Able to leap tall buildings in a single bound! Heroes come in all shapes and sizes, personalities and passions.

These heroes for this theme are brave, thoughtful, and always willing to help others. They may not have superpowers, but they use their innate human strengths to improve the lives of others. They never have alter-egos, they are themselves. Some are loud and extrovert and some are not. Some are quiet heroes, yet they still live a heroic life.

Among these diverse heroes, this theme focuses on the quiet ones, those who make a significant difference without drawing attention to themselves.

There is often no rhyme or reason to what happens in life. The only choice we have is how we choose to respond. Quiet heroes choose to respond to the hand of cards that life played, to being the most kind and reliable people they can be.

This theme is for those people who have their own battles to fight, but set those feeling, hurts or physical challenges aside to fight the cause of others. They are strong in who they are, comfy in their own skin. Often are kind, and always putting other people first. Not arrogant and boasting, modest about their achievements.

It's quite normal these people do not know how much of a hero they are. For most quiet heroes are not aware of the impact they make as they walk through the world, but leave a trail of changed lives in their footsteps.

***

# Title: What A Ride!

Quotation by Hunter S. Thompson

'Life should not be a journey to the grave with the intention of arriving safely in a pretty and well-preserved body. But rather, to skid in broadside in a cloud of smoke, thoroughly used up, totally worn out, and loudly proclaiming, "Wow! What a Ride!"

**Eulogy themes.**

- Adventure.
- Risk.
- Exploration.
- Speed.
- Charisma.
- Daring.

**Character Descriptions**

Some people live life to the fullest. Looking for fresh adventures or exploring different places. Taking risks for a rush. Motorbikes, bungee jumping, skydiving, scuba diving - that's their life.

It may be in their 90s learning to fly a passenger jet flight simulator. Or joining an exercise class.

With no shadow of a doubt, some live life on their terms and in their ways, even if it means their life ends sooner than expected. Their legacy is of a person who was never short of a smile, a laugh, a joke, a drink in their hand, perhaps, and a party to go to. Always with a smile on their face.

The same level of risk could also be in starting a business. An entrepreneur with a vision to reach, selling everything to start a new life. The exude confidence and charisma. Age or circumstances never hold them back. For them, age is merely a number.

These people are often outgoing, flamboyant, funny, and generous. Often called, 'One in a Million.' Loud, cheeky, and a party animal. Completely proud of living the life they wanted.

These are stories that need to be told. It reminds us all we have one chance to live the life we want, regardless of others' opinions or choices.

# Chapter 31

## BONUS WORKSHEET 4 – 36 EXTRA MEMORY PROMPT QUESTIONS

IT'S CHALLENGING TO BRING to mind lots of details about someone's life. If I say to you, 'Tell me about this person', where do you start? How can you try to answer that question?

These 36 extra memory prompts will bring to mind stories and sayings and help you describe the personality and character they had. What made them unique?

They will help make the eulogy you write personal and relevant, as others who hear your words too will recognise these same key themes in the person's life.

It can be quite challenging to read through and answer some of these questions, so take your time. Don't do it all in one sitting. There will be some questions easier to answer than others. Some may come to you instantly. Others will take some reflection. Some questions might bring to the surface emotions of all kinds. Other questions may not apply.

What will make your words memorable and helpful for you and those listening will be the specific way you describe the person. Doing this will resonate and you'll find people saying, 'Yes, that's the person I remember, love and miss.'

**Childhood and Early Years:**

What funny stories did they tell of growing up?

Where did they go to school and did they enjoy those days? Why?

How would they describe their childhood?

What would have been their favourite memory of their childhood?

How did those early days shape the person they would become?

**Relationships and Partnerships:**

How did they meet their life partner? When and where did they meet them for the first time?

How and why were they attracted to each other? If they married, where and when did the ceremony take place?

**Character and Personality:**

Was the person funny, kind, generous, family-orientated, intelligent, hard-working or easy-going?

Were they a 'life and soul of the party' person?

Were they shy, private, and reserved?

How did their personality make them unique and memorable?

What quirky traits, like being punctual or always late, tidy or messy, did they have?

Did they have any memorable catchphrases or sayings?

Was there a distinctive smell you associate with them? (Aftershave or perfume, pipe smoke or baking bread?)

How would you describe their sense of humour? Were they witty with one-liners, or did they tell funny stories?

**Professional Life:**

What was their work or career path?

What were their skills and talents? Such as an engineer, homemaker, leader or artist?

What were their greatest successes and achievements?

What were the greatest struggles and challenges they faced?

Did any significant events or decisions change their life's direction?

**Personal Preferences and Interests:**

What books did they read, and who was their favourite author?

Did they have a favourite quote they liked?

Which music was their first choice?

Did they have an artist or group they enjoyed or followed?

How did they spend leisure time?

What hobbies did they enjoy?

What were their most cherished possessions?

Did they collect or 'hoard' anything?

**Community Involvement:**

Did they volunteer or serve in the community?

To which groups or organisations did they belong?

Did they donate to any charities?

In which ways were they altruistic?

**Memorable Experiences and Reflections:**

What memorable experiences did they have in life, like travel or adventures?

What memorable experiences did you share?

Looking back over their life, what were the happiest years?

What will you miss most about them?

# Chapter 32

## BONUS WORKSHEET 5 – 26 QUOTATIONS FOR TELLING A LIFE STORY

HAVING WRITTEN OVER 700 eulogies, I've had the privilege and honour to look into people's unique, extraordinary life stories. Every person has a tale worth telling, and it's been my privilege to find and write them. Some are easier to find than others. But there is a life story worth telling in everyone.

Finding a suitable quote to use as a hook when you start your words, or as an illustration, might be something you could use. So here are a few of the quotes I have used in eulogies over the years.

Thank you to all the authors who have penned these words, giving their creativity to make the world beautiful for others.

Use them if you can, but always use and give due recognition to the original author.

1. 'I don't want to get to the end of my life and find that I just lived the length of it. I want to live the width of it as well.' Diane Ackerman.

2. 'Every man dies. Not every man really lives.' William Wallace.

3. 'Often the difference between a successful person and a failure is not one's better abilities or ideas, but the courage that one has to bet on one's ideas, to take a calculated risk—and to act.' André Malraux.

4. 'Yours is the light by which my spirit's born: - you are my sun, my moon, and all my stars.' E. E. Cummings.

5. 'To the world you may be one person but to one person you may be the world.' Bill Wilson

6. 'I could not tell you if I loved you the first moment I saw you, or if it was the second or third or fourth. But I remember the first moment I looked at you walking toward me and realised that somehow the rest of the world seemed to vanish when I was with you.' Cassandra Clare.

7. 'So much of what is best in us is bound up in our love of family, that it remains the measure of our stability because it measures our sense of loyalty.' Haniel Long.

8. 'If you are going to achieve excellence in big things, you develop the habit in little matters. Excellence is not an exception, it is a prevailing attitude.' Colin Powell.

9. 'The strength of a man is in his character. A strong man is a great man of wisdom who understands his top priority is to his family.' Ellen J. Barrier.

10. 'Sharing tales of those we've lost is how we keep from really losing them.' Mitch Albom.

11. 'The purpose of life is to live it, to taste experience to the utmost, to reach out eagerly and without fear for newer and richer experience.' Eleanor Roosevelt.

12. 'This is part of what a family is about, not just love. It's knowing that your family will be there watching out for you. Nothing else will give you that. Not money. Not fame. Not work.' Mitch Albom.

13. 'I am content; that is a blessing greater than riches; and he to whom that is given need ask no more.' Henry Fielding

14. 'Resilience is accepting your new reality, even if it's less good than the one you had before. You can fight it, you can do nothing but scream about what you've lost, or you can accept that and try to put together something that's good.' Elizabeth Edwards.

15. 'If you have strength of character, you can use that as fuel to not only be a survivor, but to transcend simply being a survivor, use an internal alchemy to turn something rotten and horrible into gold.' Zeena Schreck.

16. 'I can be changed by what happens to me. But I refuse to be reduced by it.' Maya Angelou.

17. 'Life changes in the instant. The ordinary instant.' Joan Didion.

18. 'In the end, only three things matter: how much you loved, how gently you lived, and how gracefully you let go of things not meant for you.' Jack Kornfield.

19. 'You give but little when you give of your possessions. It is when you give of yourself that you truly give.' Kahlil Gibran.

20. 'The most truly generous persons are those who give silently without hope of praise or reward.' Carol Ryrie Brink.

21. 'Do your little bit of good where you are; it's those little bits of good put together that

overwhelm the world.' Desmond Tutu.

22. 'Attitude is a choice. Happiness is a choice. Optimism is a choice. Kindness is a choice. Giving is a choice. Respect is a choice. Whatever choice you make makes you. Choose wisely.' Roy T. Bennett.

23. 'Life becomes easier and more beautiful when we can see the good in other people.' Roy T. Bennett.

24. 'Let us be grateful to the people who make us happy; they are the charming gardeners who make our souls blossom.' Marcel Proust.

25. 'I hold that a strongly marked personality can influence descendants for generations.' Beatrix Potter.

26. 'A gentleman is one who puts more into the world than he takes out.' George Bernard Shaw.

# Chapter 33

## BONUS WORKSHEET 6 – FAMILY & FRIENDS QUESTIONNAIRE

**Example letter or email to send to a family member or friend.**

HI BARRY,

It's hard to believe I'm writing this email. I never thought the day would come. Somehow, I imagined he would be here forever. But the funeral is fast approaching, and I want to say a few words at dad's service. I wanted to ask a few people who knew my dad, Alan, some questions about him to help me give a full picture of his life. Would you be willing to help me, please?

Here are some questions which may prompt some memories. If you could send me any thoughts, stories or memories, I would be so grateful. While I may not say everything in my few words, the more I can build a complete picture of dad, the more my words will help everyone there.

How would you describe Alan's personality: was he quiet, reserved and private or outgoing, loud and a life and soul of the party person or something else? In what way did these traits show themselves?

- What was he skilled at doing? What were his talents and abilities, would you say?

- Did Alan have any quirky traits that you might remember with a smile?

- What are the top three things Alan enjoyed doing?

- Who were his closest friends, past and present? What kinds of things did they do together?

- Was there some expression unique to him?

- How would you describe his sense of humour? Was it witty with one-liners, or did he tell funny stories?

- If you could only say three things about him, what would they be?

- How do you think he would like to be remembered?

Are there any other things you think would be important to mention about him in describing his life that I haven't asked?

Thank you very much for your help in sending me any information about him.

With grateful thanks,

# Notes

# Notes

# Notes

# Notes

# Notes

# Chapter 34

## BESPOKE EULOGY WRITING SOLUTIONS

**Discover a Path to Honouring Your Loved One's Funeral with A Bespoke Eulogy Writing Solution**

**Your Journey, Your Choice: From Do It Yourself to a Do It For You Bespoke Personal Service**

Losing a loved one is an emotional journey, and I believe honouring their life should be a personal and thoughtful process. That's why I've created a range of options to support you in crafting a eulogy that genuinely reflects their unique life and legacy.

1. **Do It Yourself**: This comprehensive workbook provides the guidance you need to write a heartfelt eulogy. It's not only about the words, but about weaving together cherished memories and emotions into a meaningful tribute.

2. **Do It Together:** If you feel the need for a supportive hand, I offer a review service where you and I can work together. This collaborative process ensures your self-written eulogy becomes a touching tribute, complete with expert advice, rewrites, and enhancements.

3. **Do It For You: A Bespoke Eulogy Writing Solution:** If you feel overwhelmed by the task and need a helping hand, I can craft a unique, personalised eulogy for you, providing comfort and assurance during your challenging time.

**Why Choose My Bespoke Eulogy Writing Service?**

Online templates may be quick, but they often miss capturing the essence of your loved one's life. My bespoke service offers a distinct approach, focusing on personalisation, understanding, and care.

<u>Here's what sets this service apart:</u>

- **Personal Touch:** I believe that every life is unique and deserves a unique tribute. I listen intently to your stories and memories, crafting them into a eulogy that genuinely reflects your loved one's qualities, experiences, and connections.

- **Depth of Emotion:** I aim to create a eulogy that recounts not only a life but also articulates the impact your loved one had on those around them.

- **Resonance:** My bespoke service ensures that the eulogy resonates with everyone present, celebrating your loved one's life truly meaningfully.

**The Bespoke Eulogy Writing Process**

The detailed bespoke service includes:

- A memory prompt questionnaire.

- A 1-hour phone or video call to understand your loved one's story.

- A custom written eulogy, 3 A4 pages long (around 1300-1500 words).

- Speaking time of 8-12 minutes to ensure a comprehensive tribute.

- Unlimited rewrites for absolute satisfaction.

- First Draft Delivery within 4 working days*.

- Option to expedite the process with 2 or 1 Working Day Delivery*.

*Please note - first draft delivery times are from receipt of memory prompt questionnaires and/or 1:1 telephone or video call.

**I'm Here to Help**

Whether you choose to use this workbook alone, collaborate, or prefer me to write the eulogy, I'm dedicated to helping you honour your loved one in the most heartfelt way.

For more information, visit the website at - https://www.memorablewords.co.uk/eulogy-writing-services or email me info@memorablewords.co.uk.

**Remember, every life has a story. Let me help you tell it.**

# Testimonials for Peter Billingham Eulogy Speechwriter and Celebrant

### 'The eulogy he wrote for our mom was just perfect in every way.'

From the very first telephone conversation with Pete, I can say he has a calming influence, which, in turn, made an extremely sad and upsetting experience a little easier to cope with. The eulogy he wrote for our mom was just perfect in every way. Can we express our gratitude to you Pete for the celebration of mom's life, that touched everyone in a way that will, and has bought comfort to all... Les Chance – Google 5-star Review

### 'Peter wrote a beautiful, heartfelt, and sincere eulogy.'

Peter is kind, caring, and compassionate. From our first conversation, he put me at ease, making a very daunting and difficult time a lot easier. He spent a lot of time speaking and listening to me, getting to know about my mom and wrote a beautiful, heartfelt and sincere eulogy, adding his own personal touches that made it so special and unique... I would highly recommend him. Thank you so much Peter. Stephanie Marsh – Google 5-star Review

### 'The words Peter had used truly reflected the man they knew and loved.'

I can't thank Peter enough for the eulogy he composed for my dad. We shared stories and memories with Peter in the hope that he would in some way be able to understand the person dad was. Not only did we feel Peter understood him, but it felt as though he knew him well. We had guests request copies of the eulogy because they felt that the words Peter had used truly reflected the man they knew and loved. Rachel Clements – Google 5-star Review

### 'I HIGHLY recommend Peter and his services...'

I am very happy that I found Peter and his services. I am ever happier with the final results that Peter delivered through his online memorial services. Peter put together the written and spoken package service for my best friend, one of the people that I care most about in this world. Peter is patient (SO patient), kind, caring, and really did a great deal of work into putting together something that really displayed the wonderful man that meant so much to me and so many others. I am grateful for the amazing service... His response time with communication was very quick despite our time difference since I am in the United States. I HIGHLY recommend Peter and his services... Peter, I appreciate everything you did for us. Your time, effort and care really shows in the final results. I can't thank you enough!

Chris Johnson – Google 5-star Review

## 'I would use 100% Peter's services again - cannot recommend him highly enough.'

My experience of using Peter's services was better than I thought. My father had passed away, and we were getting closer to his funeral. The problem was that I was struggling to put what was in my head onto paper, so after going on the internet, I came across Peter and used his fantastic eulogy services.

The whole process was very helpful. We used the service where you get a video chat that made it so much easier when my mother and I sat with Peter on a video call recalling stories. When we had a finished eulogy which lasted about 8 mins was better than I could have wished.

Also, Peter talks you through the best way to approach reading and talks in a calm manner, which helped me to deliver my dad's eulogy. I would 100% use Peters services again cannot recommend him highly enough. Darren Evans – Google 5-star Review

## 'Pete had the incredible ability to capture the essence of my late Dad's real character...'

Pete had the incredible ability to capture the essence of my late Dad's real character through carefully constructed questions and an informal. Friendly, face-to-face chat over a cup of tea. He delivered his carefully crafted eulogy with the warmth of a lifelong friend. We felt Pete knew and respected my Dad, without ever having met him. Absolutely the right person for such an important role. Thank you Pete! David Glasbey - Google 5-star Review

Read these and over 90 5 Star ***** reviews of Peter's work as a professional eulogy speechwriter and celebrant via Google Reviews.

# Chapter 35

## ACKNOWLEDGEMENTS

CRAFTING THIS BOOK HAS been a journey of not only personal growth but also of deepened understanding as I have tried to bring to the pages ten years of experience as a eulogy speechwriter and celebrant. I have been fortunate to have an incredible group of people who walked this path with me, and I am sincerely grateful for their support.

Foremost, my heartfelt thanks go to my daughter, Laura Stroud. Her encouragement, insightful feedback on early drafts, and her advice on the book cover have been invaluable. Laura, your joy and passion for writing is a constant source of inspiration. To Alex Davis, your patience and constructive feedback improved this work immeasurably. I am deeply grateful for your support. To Mark Sheldon, your thoughtful insights as a beta reader shaped this book in many ways. Thank you.

I extend my gratitude to GetCovers, whose patience and skill in creating the book cover and marketing support materials have helped to take my ideas and make them a reality.

To the funeral directors who recommended me to grieving families over the last decade, thank you for your trust and confidence in my ability as a eulogy speechwriter and celebrant.

The core of this book is the individuals and families who opened their hearts and lives to me. To those who trusted me to write eulogies for their loved ones, and to the hundreds of individuals whose lives I have had the honour and privilege of commemorating - this book is a testament to you. You have shown me the power of words and the strength of the human spirit in times of profound loss.

To all those who want to say a few words at a funeral but don't know where to start, I hope this book bridges the gap between the overwhelming desire to speak and the way to write the words. Thank you for trusting me to guide you through this process.

# Chapter 36

## ABOUT THE AUTHOR

PETER BILLINGHAM IS A highly recognised eulogy speechwriter. With over 700 eulogies to his name, his story-centred approach crafts memorable words that capture the essence of a loved one. Listening to hundreds of life stories, Peter understands at a deep level those moments that make our lives memorable.

Peter has authored several books, including his latest work, Gathering Rosebuds in Kerala, A Memoir About Storing Life's Special Moments. This thought-provoking memoir explores a 60th birthday journey to South India, reflections on ageing, discovering life's meaning, and cherishing special moments forever. Readers can also benefit from a free accompanying workbook teaching them how to craft their life stories.

Beyond his writing, Peter's passions are as diverse as they are engaging. His Golden Retriever is an ever-loyal shadow. Owning a dog has been part of life since he can't remember when.

His passion for travel is unabated. The joy of packing a suitcase has seen him visit forty-one countries so far for pleasure and in working across the world for an international charity.

Peter is an avid walker. He trekked the scenic Camino French Way, covering 780 km, alongside his best friend. Together, they journeyed from St. Jean-Pied-De-Port in France, across the Pyrenees, through the La Rioja wine region (home to his favourite wine), and along the rolling hills of northern Spain, culminating in Santiago de Compostela. Peter also completed the Camino Portugues Coastal route, a 280 km walk from Porto, this time accompanied by his children, creating lasting memories for them all.

His interests also extend to music, where he's currently learning to play acoustic blues on a Gretsch Guitar. Sore fingers and frustrated picking, but he loves the challenge of learning new skills.

His creativity spills over into his collaboration with his daughter, Laura Stroud, in developing Derbyshire Writing School. Their warm and engaging 'dad and daughter' podcast, called Begin, shares writing skills with listeners across the world.

As a member of U3A, Peter plays lawn green bowls during the summer, enjoying the friendly competition and camaraderie it offers. Additionally, he's delving into the science of longevity, always eager to learn and apply knowledge to improve his work and personal life.

Peter is a man who fills his life with varied experiences, each enriching his perspective and adding depth to his writings. He invites you to connect with him and learn more about his work at www.peterbillingham.com.

# Chapter 37

## Disclaimer

THIS PUBLICATION IS DESIGNED to provide accurate and authoritative information in regard to the subject matter covered.

It is sold or given away for free with the understanding that neither the author nor the publisher is engaged in rendering legal, investment, accounting, or other professional services.

While the publisher and author have used their best efforts in preparing this book, they make no representations or warranties with respect to the accuracy or completeness of the contents of this book and specifically disclaim any implied warranties of merchantability or fitness for a particular purpose.

No warranty may be created or extended by sales representatives or written sales materials. The advice and strategies contained herein may not be suitable for your situation. You should consult with a professional when appropriate.

Neither the publisher nor the author shall be liable for any loss of profit or any other commercial damages, including but not limited to special, incidental, consequential, personal or other damages.

No portion of this book may be reproduced in any form without written permission from the publisher or author, except as permitted by U.S. and UK copyright law.

All logos, trademarks and registered trademarks are the property of their respective owners.

The reader should not consider this book anything other than a work of non-fiction literature.

Any external website links are only for reference. Content from any such articles may have changed or removed without the author's knowledge. Links to free downloads and book offers are not guaranteed to be accessible in perpetuity. The author will try to correct errors brought to their attention.

Product renderings are examples of what the product may look like on a device, or when printed. The monitors, tablets, eReader devices and printed versions of the materials are not included in any purchase.

www.ingramcontent.com/pod-product-compliance
Lightning Source LLC
Chambersburg PA
CBHW040124130526
44591CB00040B/2931